STUCK FOR
WORDS
WHAT TO SAY TO
SOMEONE WHO IS GRIEVING

www.wilkinsonpublishing.com.au

Published by:
Wilkinson Publishing Pty Ltd
ACN 006 042 173
Level 4, 2 Collins Street
Melbourne, Vic 3000
Ph: 03 9654 5446
www.wilkinsonpublishing.com.au

Design: Lee Walker

National Library of Australia Cataloguing-in-Publication entry
Creator: Zagdanski, Doris, 1954- author.
Title: Stuck for words : what to say to someone who is grieving / Doris Zagdanski.
ISBN: 9781925642001 (paperback)
Subjects: Grief--Psychological aspects.
Bereavement--Psychological aspects.
Death--Psychological aspects.
Consolation.

ABOUT THE AUTHOR

Doris Zagdanski has had the opportunity to meet hundreds of grieving people. She has volunteered her time as a Home Visitor to families in Victoria whose child died unexpectedly from Sudden Infant Death Syndrome and is well known to many support groups for the bereaved. She has worked on the front line as a funeral director and is still employed in the funeral industry.

For the past 30 years, her career has centered on grief education throughout Australia and overseas.

She is the author of seven books on loss, grief and empathy and is a sought after conference speaker and trainer in her field – her message about grief is contemporary, educational, entertaining and real.

CONTENTS

Introduction   1

Chapter 1   Am I qualified to help?   5

Chapter 2   A closer look at grief   13

Chapter 3   Where there's loss, there's grief   25

Chapter 4   Should I bring up the subject?   31

Chapter 5   How are you? ... And then what do I say?   38

Chapter 6   Listening first, then empathy   45

Chapter 7   What exactly is empathy?   54

Chapter 8   Will faith fix it?   67

Chapter 9   When do you call in professional help?   75

Chapter 10   How long will all this grieving last?   91

Chapter 11   What about children?   100

Chapter 12   Empathy is also about your actions   112

Chapter 13   Over to you – how would you respond with empathy?   122

Bibliography   149

Acknowledgements   152

INTRODUCTION

The first edition of *Stuck For Words* was published in 1994. Part of my motivation for writing this book came from my own life experience. This is how I explained it in the original version:

> *In 1980, the quiet routine of my family's life was changed in an instant by the sudden and unexplained death of Claire, our two month old daughter. The cause? "Consistent with Sudden Infant Death Syndrome", said the Coroner's report. I remember many things about the nightmare of the days, weeks, months, and more months which followed. But there's something else I also remember – the things people said.*

> *The courageous ones actually addressed what happened; some even said the word d-e-a-d: Sorry to hear that your baby died. The not-so-brave didn't mention the subject at all or simply stayed away. But the ones who really got to me were the would-be magicians, those who thought our grief would vanish into thin air if they offered some magic words like:*

> *Don't cry, you can have more kids.*
>
> *It could have been worse, at least she didn't suffer.*
>
> *She's lucky. She's with God now.*

> *Since then, my work has enabled me to meet hundreds of grieving people whose lives were somehow changed by loss and eventually we would always end up asking that same question: Why do people think they have to cheer you up when something goes wrong in your life?*

With this revised version, there comes an obvious question: "Are we any better at talking to grieving people at this point in time, more than twenty years later?"

Here are some considerations to help answer this question. Social media has provided us with a swift and easily accessible way to communicate when there is a tragedy – either public or personal. Condolence pages through Facebook or other memorial websites are now a common way of expressing your thoughts and feelings.

So, if you know someone who is grieving, it's acceptable to send them a text message, "like" their Facebook post (even if it says their mother has just died!) and leave a comment if you wish – all part of the modern way we now talk to each other.

The internet is also a huge source of information on any topic related to loss and grief – words like suicide, stillbirth and cancer are not taboo on the internet. There is a plethora of information at our fingertips – from research papers to personal blogs, from support groups to factsheets – the topics of death, loss and grief are now well and truly open for discussion.

There are wide reaching networks of support these days – government agencies, community support groups, mental health services and the like. National and international calendars of awareness days now exist – Pink Ribbon Day for breast cancer, White Ribbon Day for domestic violence, Red Ribbon Day for AIDS/HIV, Grey Ribbon Day for diabetes … the list is endless. Such days put the spotlight on these issues, helping us to be informed about the subject and also to consider those who are personally affected.

Prolonged Grief Disorder (PGD)[1], also known as complicated grief, pathological grief or traumatic grief put the topic of grief in the media spotlight in recent years when it was proposed that PGD be classified as a mental disorder. Whilst the deliberation continues, researchers have found that 10-20% of people have a prolonged response to bereavement that is extreme and persistent and impacts on their day to day functioning and long term health and wellness. While normal grief can be intense and painful, when your grief gets complicated, it remains heightened, it's all you can focus on and leaves you feeling that life has no purpose or meaning anymore.

An Australian study[2], published in 2015, looked at bereavement risk and support needs in the community. With a sample of 678 respondents, one of the aims was to screen those at risk of PGD. It found that 58.4% were at low risk, 35.2% at moderate risk and 6.4% were high risk. What is interesting to note is that all three groups of grievers looked to family and friends for support, the moderate risk group may have also sought help from support groups and agencies such as palliative care services whilst the high risk group reported more frequent help was sought from mental health experts[3].

It all boils down to this. When we are grieving we tend to rely on our family and friends for support and comfort. They are the obvious ones we turn to. They are the front line of support. We think they'll know what to say and do. So if we find they fall short, it can leave us feeling disappointed and hurt – and that means more grief to deal with. A bereaved father described his own situation like this:

My own family and friends, as well as my workmates were awkwardly sympathetic. I suppose I would have liked more of them to have 'fronted me' with their sympathy, rather than implying by their respectful distance that they indeed cared.

I talk to grieving people almost every day. And one thing has not changed over the years. Invariably the subject of what someone said that puzzled or upset them still comes up. As long as there are people around who truly believe that *time will heal* or *God did this for a reason* or *it's best to be brave and not cry*, grieving people will continue to feel misunderstood and alone.

Conversations will become awkward and friendships will become strained. This means that grieving people are often forced to put on a brave face rather than be themselves. Friends may cross the street or just not visit like they used to – not because they don't care, they just don't know how to make an approach. They don't know how to use the power of empathy to connect with their friend.

Here's the challenge for us — whilst a text message from a friend lets you know you are being remembered, the art of having a face to face conversation may become a thing of the past if we rely on social media to do our talking.

According to internationally known Vietnamese monk, author and scholar Thich Nhat Hanh[4], we need to practice looking deeply into another person if we wish to fully understand them. To have compassion with their pain requires us to have the *ability to understand their pain*, not just the *desire* to help ease it. Allowing a grieving person to tell their story and knowing how to respond effectively – not just to their words but their feelings as well – is the art of empathy. This is one way to clearly show our compassion, our understanding of their pain.

Knowing that you don't have to fix their grief or say something philosophical to make it seem right underpin the essence of an empathetic response. If we can keep a conversation flowing even when there's talk of anger, blame, despair, disbelief, regret ... we occupy a significant place in a relationship that frightens most people, even friends who really care about us.

One thing I've noticed is that there is no queue at your front door when you are grieving – once the funeral is over, so are most of your visitors. You might underestimate just how welcome you are when you turn up at your friend's front door armed with the helping strategies and conversation tools in this book. The emphasis throughout is that when someone like you makes an approach to talk to a grieving person, you are in fact engaging in the task of helping. So from now on, I will refer to you as 'the helper'.

Believe me, the bereaved know it's not easy to be in your shoes, but your involvement in their grief – what you say and what you do, will have a substantial effect on how their grief turns out. Your willingness to talk about what's happened can actually make a difference to the way someone deals with death or any other life changing event. Inviting a friend to tell you their story may be one of the most helpful things you can do.

> *"There is no greater agony than bearing an untold story inside you."*
> *Maya Angelou*

CHAPTER 1

AM I QUALIFIED TO HELP?

"My best friend's husband has just dropped dead and I don't know what to do."

"Since my sister-in-law's baby died she's just not the same. How can I get her to snap out of it?"

"Dad's been moping around for weeks now since Mum died. What can we do to cheer him up?"

Help! That's what these statements are really saying. Help me, so that I can help someone else. If you find yourself in the position of having to visit, work with, comfort or just chat to someone who is grieving, you are occupying the role of a helper – whether you are trained or not, whether you know what to say or not, whether you feel comfortable or not.

Since talking about death is still considered a no-no by many people, the resulting problem is that talking about feelings has become difficult too. Often in the aftermath of a crisis, let's say a death in the family, people swing into action and provide assistance which is largely practical and organisational. Help takes on the form of *activity* – making funeral arrangements, telephoning relatives, preparing meals and perhaps caring for young children. But sooner or later the emphasis will shift to the subject of feelings and they have to be dealt with too. This is where help takes on the form of *being* – being with someone who is emotional – sad, angry, guilty, bitter, hostile, frustrated or helpless. Even though the topic of "feelings" is a frightening area for many, it won't go away just because it makes you uncomfortable.

You might think that you are not trained for this. After all, we have professionals to do this kind of job. But even amongst the "helping professions" – counsellors, psychologists, psychiatrists, doctors, nurses, social workers, funeral directors and allied health services, it is personal qualities, not academic qualifications that determine their effectiveness. In many instances, it's not the professionals but rather the person in the street who ends up being the one the bereaved turn to. And it makes sense. Friends, neighbours, workmates and people who they see every day are the obvious ones who are in a position to talk about what has happened. So these people become part of the network of *informal* helpers who have the potential to be a kind of lifebuoy to a friend who is temporarily swamped by the wave of reactions and emotions which are termed 'grief'.

There is an assumption that it may be best not to interfere in something as private or as personal as grief. Or, you might presume that there are enough relatives around to support each other – *It's the family's job ... She has her children close by ... I'll only get in the way.* It's worth mentioning though that sometimes family members choose not to share all, or any, of their feelings and concerns with each other. Not only may they have different responses to the same loss, but it seems they may be trying to shield each other from extra hurt by keeping their feelings to themselves. So here is your opportunity to be available to your friend, when they want to talk to someone who is close enough to share the problem but is not directly affected themselves.

Another common belief about loss is that unless you've been through it yourself you really can't understand how someone else is feeling. If this were true, then professional counsellors would have to have been widowed, divorced, assaulted, retrenched or experienced all other possible woes of their clients, otherwise we would conclude that they would be of no help at all. This just isn't the case.

More important than *who* you are is *how* you are in the company of your grieving friend. The most accurate indicator of your helpfulness will be your ability to show you are trying to understand how your friend is feeling. When people are grieving, they need to know that those around them understand – even though they have changed, even though they don't laugh as much anymore, even though they start to cry right in the middle of doing their shopping and can't explain why.

There is so much relief in finding others who are willing to hear you tell your story even if they have never been there themselves. This will only happen though, when you, the helper, are able to communicate acceptance of 'how it is' for another human who is in the midst of a personal crisis. This communication is central to the whole task of helping.

"When I'm really down, I usually cry alone. At work they think I'm 'all better', but this clever charade is only because I've found so few people who want you around if you're always sad."

Grieving is not an easy thing to do in our society. At least not openly, in front of others. We have inherited the idea that a person ought not to cry or talk about their feelings and so we applaud those who are outwardly grief-free and hold up well in a crisis. Labels such as "not coping", "fallen in a heap" or "a mess" describe the rest!

In my work as a funeral director, I rarely heard people say: *"You know, Mum really cried when the doctor told her that Dad didn't make it. I'm glad she let it all out like that."* This becomes the challenge for helpers and the wider community – to be able to change their perception from believing that grieving is weak or self-indulgent to understanding that it has a purpose and is a necessary function – physically, psychologically and spiritually.

In his book, *Talking About Death*[5] , Graeme Griffin described a study which was carried out several years ago on the effects of grief on some hundreds of widows. Conducted by Professor David Maddison of Sydney University, the research looked at the impact of grief on the physical health of these widows during the first twelve months of bereavement. In brief, he found that a little over one third of the widows fell moderately ill, almost one third fell seriously ill and one third did not become ill. You might well ask, as did Professor Maddison, what was it that protected the one third who did not fall ill? Did they have children to care for or jobs to go to? Was it a lack of financial worries? Did their age make any difference? Or did their religious beliefs keep them going? Griffin takes up the story saying:

The one thing that could be distinguished between the widows who stayed well and those who fell ill was that the women who stayed well found someone who allowed them to do their grieving; someone who didn't say "don't cry"; someone who allowed them to express the feelings they genuinely had. It was not a matter of having to do something for them; it was rather a matter of allowing something in them to come out.

It is clear that friends, who offer *shoulds* and *oughts*, or messages which imply the bereaved are wrong to feel the way they do, are themselves on the wrong track. Helpers are not responsible for curing grief yet they are capable of making the whole experience a little, sometimes even a lot, easier to bear.

The next requirement is the right attitude, summed up with the words *genuineness* and *respect*. [6] A genuine helper is not nosey, intrusive or a busy-body and is available well beyond the offer of words like, "if there is anything I can do, just give me a call". Respect for grieving people is conveyed by allowing them to show their feelings without judgement or ridicule and by accepting differences in their creed, culture and the way they express themselves.

To be an effective helper also means tackling society's general perception about the whole subject of death, dying and feelings. For many people these are still prohibited topics of conversation. When words like 'dead', 'cancer' or 'suicide' are whispered, we make it so much harder for those affected to talk about what's happened. One way we can all begin to feel more comfortable with the whole idea of talking about feelings, is to rid ourselves of the notion that it's a scary subject.

It's also important to know the difference between the myths and truths of grief.

Here are **20 quick tips**[7] to get you started. They cover many of the ideas which are talked about in this book.

1   **Grief is about *loss*, not death alone.** We need to allow people going through all kinds of personal problems, disappointments, hurts and life-changing events to have their grief. No point in saying, "there are others worse off" – when you're experiencing your own unwanted

or unexpected life event, you can only feel your own pain. It's valid. It's normal. It's called 'grief'.

2   **One loss usually triggers a whole lot more.** I often liken it to a jigsaw puzzle – when one piece goes missing the whole puzzle is affected and isn't held together anymore. It doesn't look the same anymore. So, when one piece of your life is changed or is "lost", other pieces like companionship, finances, friendships, holidays, mealtimes, outings, family gatherings, daily routines, and a whole lot more all change too. Learning to adapt to these changes is sometimes called your 'grief work' – and only you can do this work for yourself.

3   **Grief doesn't come in neat, consecutive stages.** In fact, there's not much about grief that's neat at all. It comes in waves, sometimes so strong that you think you're drowning in emotions. They may be scary, unfamiliar, keep you awake and stop you from eating. Many people worry and think they're going crazy. Don't expect it to be a smooth road, it just isn't.

4   **People may be quite uncomfortable around you.** Even people you know well may not know what to say or will say things that surprise you or make you mad. They think they have to cheer you up or offer you some wise words. Maybe a silent hug would be better.

5   **Time does NOT heal.** It just moves on. It's what you do with your time that creates the healing. Doing nothing doesn't make your grief go away. You can't avoid it. You can't hide from it. You need to go 'with it'. You don't get 'over it', you just adapt. And this takes a lot of time. Over time, you can learn how to adapt to what's happened and how your life has changed.

6   **Grief changes you.** A significant loss will always affect your life to such an extent that many things in your world will be different. Including you. Remember the jigsaw puzzle. So don't expect to be your old self again – grieving requires you to learn new ways of coping, learn new skills, and learn to live without someone who meant so much.

7   **There will be 'Whys?' and 'What ifs?'** Accept that some things will never make sense to you and even if you get answers, they still don't make things right or fair. The trick is to learn to live without the answers or the reasons why.

8   **Crying is coping.** It just makes others feel awkward so they often urge you to be strong and think of all your happy memories. Crying is okay and not crying is okay. But it's said that crying with someone has a better effect on you than crying alone!

9   **'Closure' is an odd concept.** It's not realistic to ask someone to 'close off' their love for someone – like you would close a bank account or close a door. These days, we say that finding ways to keep the bonds of love and friendship connected are more akin to healthy grieving.

10   **A lot of people might come to the funeral.** But it doesn't mean you'll have a lot of support. It doesn't take long before the phone stops ringing and people don't drop in. Sometimes it's because they think you have your family around or other friends will be there for you. But the truth is, the time after a funeral can be very lonely and isolating and many people avoid you because they don't know what to say. They do care, but they feel uncomfortable.

11   **Dead is NOT like sleeping.** It's about life ending. Sometimes we give children explanations of death that are confusing and not truthful. It's tempting to use words like 'gone' or 'asleep' when we actually mean 'dead'. We often do this to protect children but it doesn't really help them to understand what's happened. Or to understand why the adults are so upset and things at home are so different. Children want information, not fairy tales.

12   **People say, "If there's anything I can do just give me a call."** But they probably won't show up. Prepare to be disappointed. On the other hand, there may be people, who you least expected, who offer to help you or are just there as good listeners. Prepare to be surprised.

13 **People will have an opinion on how you are doing.** Don't gauge your grief by the way others are doing theirs. There's no roadmap to follow. People often want you to 'move on' and they never expect your grief to last as long as it does.

14 **It's okay to get angry because people say stupid things.** But it doesn't mean they don't care about you or lack compassion. They think they are saying the right thing to cheer you up and take your grief away – they think this is the right way to help you feel better.

15 **Don't dispose of personal possessions too soon.** You may think it will help the grief to go away – but it won't. You may even be urged by your family to do this. They think it will help you 'get over it' faster. Later, you may just wish you'd kept some stuff but it's too late once it's gone. And don't forget to ask the children if there's anything they would like to keep – you might be surprised what they would choose as an endearing memento.

16 **Grief can make you afraid of getting close to someone again.** Fear of losing again is very real and scary. It is said that grief is the price we pay for love. Another writer expressed it like this: *"If you choose to love, you must also have the courage to grieve."*

17 **You will not feel better straight after the funeral.** Once the protective layers of shock and numbness begin to wear off, grief feelings start to surface. You realise the person is never coming home. They will always be missing from your family. Some people describe it as an amputation – a part of them has died too. Now the reality is starting to sink in, accompanied by the grief that goes with it. So don't rush the funeral. Take your time to plan it carefully.

18 **Even when death is expected, it still seems sudden when it happens.** You might think you're prepared but you find nothing can really prepare you for that moment. Even if you've said your goodbyes, you may still wish you'd said or done more.

19 **People will say, "I know how you feel."** But they don't! They mean well. They even think this is how they show their empathy towards you, but words like this just get added to your list of annoying things that people say when they don't know what to say.

20 **It's okay to laugh when you're grieving.** It's okay to be relieved after someone has died. It's okay to see the imperfections in your loved one – you're not being disloyal. It's okay to be angry at the dead person for leaving you. It's okay to do and say things that you later think were crazy. This is simply the way we might feel when we are grieving. Cut yourself some slack. There's no perfect way to grieve.

CHAPTER 1

AT A GLANCE

*   Helping is not limited to the work of a professional counsellor. A friend who is willing to help, to enter into another's struggle, is like a lifebuoy. Someone to cling to until you feel strong enough to swim alone.

*   As potential helpers, we may be limited by our own fears:
    - fear of death
    - fear of talking about a touchy subject
    - fear of being inadequate
    - fear of making someone upset
    - fear of our own emotions coming out

*   You don't have to be widowed or have lost a child, parent, brother or sister to be a useful helper. It can make a difference to your awareness but it is still not a prerequisite. Genuineness and respect are the real starting point.

*   The task of helping is not concerned with categorising, changing or curing someone's feelings. It's about understanding and accepting how it is for them.

CHAPTER 2

A CLOSER LOOK AT GRIEF

If you're going to be of any help to a grieving friend, you'll need to arm yourself with some basic knowledge about grief. You see, this is where so many would-be helpers go wrong right from the start – they just don't know what real grief is about.

I was shocked and devastated, couldn't believe she'd died, confused, numb and angry.

It's a mixture of being alone and cold and lost.

It's a heavy feeling – you just drag yourself along.

The most common grievance I hear from grieving people about their family and friends, is that no-one understands what they are really going through. The key word here is 'really' – there are so many myths around about grief, that real grief is often misunderstood. There seems to be a notion that grief is about crying, feeling down and being upset. That's supposed to last for a while, probably a few months, and then you will be your old self again. But real grief doesn't work that way. I believe that you are never the same after someone close to you has died. At least one aspect, and usually many more of your life will be altered forever.

People cannot be replaced simply by putting new people in their place, yet grieving parents are told to "have another baby", a widow is told she's "young enough to marry again" and a teenager is expected to quickly forget a best mate because "you'll make new friends easily".

Try to think of it like a jigsaw. If you lose just one single piece, the whole picture doesn't look the same and if you take a piece from another puzzle, although it may look alike, it won't fit properly either. Even if you somehow found a piece with identical proportions – it still won't be the exact one that went missing. Sigmund Freud[8] described it like this:

We find a place for what we lose. Although we know that after such a loss the acute stage of mourning will subside, we also know that we shall remain inconsolable and will never find a substitute. No matter what may fill the gap, even if it be filled completely, it nevertheless remains something else.

When people are grieving they are making a protest about that missing piece, that gap in their lives. The protest is about the intrusion and the changes they are now facing. Some people will be noisy about their protest; they'll voice their anger, cry openly and demand answers from God or the people around them. Some may retreat and try to keep their feelings to themselves. The temptation to keep busy and not think about it at all will be an option for others.

The combination of possible reactions is almost endless. When we try to explain the workings of grief these days, there is less talk of phases and stages – we have moved on from that kind of thinking and we talk more in terms of allowing individual expression of grief. I think it is restrictive to imply that first comes shock, then sadness, followed by anger or depression or something else until you finally come out of it all and are hopefully healed.

These days, we talk more about 'managing your grief'. This means learning how to handle all the changes that grief brings to your life. But it's not about forgetting the person who has died. On the contrary, it's about allowing yourself to stay close to what they meant to you and all the things you value about them. There is an understanding that you will always be close to that person and that is okay.

The concept of 'letting go' of your loved one is also outmoded. Instead, learning how to acknowledge a loved one, year in, year out, as grief triggers follow you around, is more aligned to the way people do their natural grieving. The idea that we have 'continuing bonds'[9] with loved ones, which may change over time, allows people to speak freely about their loved ones and remember them without guilt or the fear that they should forget them in order to 'move on'.

Contemporary research[10] on grief has also identified grieving styles, saying that there is an 'intuitive' style and an 'instrumental' style. What this means is that some people, often females, are intuitive grievers – they are expressive of how it feels to grieve and often seek support where they can talk openly about their feelings. On the other hand, some people, often males, will tell you what they *think* about their grief, they may prefer to do something about their loss (like set up a memorial scholarship fund) rather than *talk* about how they feel.

The truth is, the way individuals manage and 'survive' a bereavement will differ from person to person. Their grief response is affected by variables which will act as clues to make your help more effective. When you talk to someone who is grieving, listen for the following information:

- What was unique about the relationship between this person and the one who died?

- What were the positives and the negatives?

- How close was the attachment? This is something that is often overlooked. Attachment is not limited to sharing a long life together or how many years you've known someone. Being 'attached' to the pending birth of a child, to a lover, to a marriage or relationship that's ended, to an anticipated way of life – all of this creates a great sense of loss and grief when it ends.

- What were the circumstances of the death – was it sudden, untimely or expected?

- How was the news broken? Was there time to say goodbye?

- Does the person have sensitive people to rely on for support by way of family, friends, church, colleagues, a doctor, employer or social network?

- How does this person usually handle stressful situations – do they clam up or communicate easily; are they open to offers of help; do they have a range of positive coping strategies to put into action or do they block out reality with alcohol, drugs or a frenzied pace of activity? Are there pre-existing mental health issues?

- Has this event come at a time when this person has other personal crises to deal with? Could they become overloaded with emotions? Could there be too much happening all at once?
- Is there unresolved grief? Are there other losses somewhere in the past that have been swept under the carpet and may therefore affect the grief that's come up now?

From this list, you can see that the significance of this present loss will be best understood by someone who is able to see the big picture and view the grief from as many angles as possible. This could mean that you witness an extensive range of grief reactions – some expected, some intense, some short term, some even appearing strange to outsiders.

Here are some possible thoughts, behaviours, feelings and reactions which are commonly considered as 'normal grief'. Remember there is no set order to experience these in. The list is only useful as a guide to establish that grief like this is not unusual.

SHOCK, DISBELIEF & NUMBNESS

My mind can't take it all in. My body seems to be on 'auto pilot'.
I'm in a daze. I can't believe it's true.

ANGER

It's not fair. I hate God. Why did this happen to our family?
How could you leave me and the kids?

DEPRESSION

I don't care anymore. Why bother getting up in the morning?
I'll never get over this. I wish I were dead too.

PANIC

How will I cope on my own? Who's going to pay the bills?
What if I drop my bundle? I'm too scared to go out by myself.

REJECTION

How could he do this to me, leaving me all on my own? Where is God now?
Where are all those friends who said they'd do anything to help?

PREOCCUPATION

I can't get my mind off this. I keep going over and over what happened.
I just can't think about anything else ... nothing else matters.
I keep wanting to talk about it and tell my story to anyone who will listen.

AGGRESSION

I feel like smashing, bashing, swearing, yelling and thumping my fists.
I want to get even. I hate the world!

GUILT & REGRETS

I just wish we hadn't had that argument.
If only I'd gone into his room earlier.
If I could just turn the clock back. I should have been a better parent.
I didn't get a chance to say goodbye.

SADNESS

I miss her so much. I feel empty inside. Will I ever smile again?
I just can't stop crying. It seems like there is a blanket of sadness over me.

INDIFFERENCE

I don't give a damn about anything anymore. I've got no motivation.
I can't be bothered hearing about everyone's problems – I've got enough of my own.

FEAR

I'm frightened to be on my own. I'm scared about seeing the coffin and all that stuff.
Night time is really scary now. What if I can't cope at the funeral?

FEELING SICK

There's a great big knot in my stomach.

My head's thumping. I'm aching all over. I'm feeling so tense in my muscles.

I just can't be bothered eating – I feel like I'm going to be sick all the time.

CONFUSION & DISORIENTATION

I can't think straight. I keep forgetting things. I can't make decisions.

I feel all mixed up. One minute I'm okay and then all of a sudden I'm a mess again.

LONELINESS

The house just feels so empty. I miss all the little things we did together.

I don't seem to fit in with my friends anymore.

There's no one to talk to.

CRYING

Should my children see me crying?

I just can't cry.

I can't go past the hospital without crying.

When I see other babies I just start to cry.

People look away when I start to cry.

Will I ever stop crying?

BITTERNESS & RESENTMENT

Why my husband? He never hurt anyone in his life.

It's not fair – God's taken my only child.

He was too young, it's just not right.

JEALOUSY

I'm so envious of other families who never have anything go wrong.

Why can't I have children like all my friends?

INSOMNIA & DREAMS

I lie awake all night … thinking. I'm too scared to go to bed at night.

I keep having dreams about what happened. She talks to me in my dreams.

LOW ENERGY

I just don't feel like going out or playing sport – I'm too tired.

I can't be bothered with the kids, they just get on my nerves. Life's a drag.

DENIAL

I don't want to hear about it. It's not true, it's not true.

I hate funerals and I'm not going. I've told myself he's just gone away for a holiday.

VOICES & VISIONS

I can hear him calling for me. I'm sure I saw him in a crowd.

WITHDRAWAL

I want to shut myself away.

Why don't you just leave me alone!

I want to run away and come back when this is all over.

LONGING & PINING

I just want my old life back. I miss her so much.

I just go over and over all the things we did together.

I'm afraid I'll forget what she looks like.

IRRITABILITY & AGITATION

I'm so annoyed with everyone's small talk, as if I care.

I can't sit still, there's too much time on my hands.

I can't stand those people who sweat the small stuff!

FRUSTRATION

It's all getting on top of me. When am I going to feel better?

Why don't people understand me?

I now have to do everything on my own – I don't know anything about shopping and cooking!

RELIEF

I'm glad all the suffering is finally over. I don't know if I could have taken much more.

We knew it would happen one day. He's been threatening to end it for years.

SUICIDAL THOUGHTS

There's no point in living without him/her. I don't have any purpose in my life now.

There's nothing but pain all around me. I can't handle this.

KEEPING BUSY

I've got to keep my mind off this. I can't sit still for one minute.

While I'm busy, I can pretend it hasn't happened.

GOING CRAZY

I've never felt like this before.

I'm so mixed up I must be going mad.

I used to be so calm about everything and now I just don't know where I'm heading.

QUESTIONING

Why me? Why him? Why her? Why not someone else? Why did God let this happen?

Why isn't there a cure for this? Why weren't our prayers answered?

Why so young?

Why? Why? Why?

EMPTINESS

I feel like something is always missing. A part of me has died.

My arms just ache to hold my child again. I feel like I'm just going through the motions of living.

IDEALISATION

He was the best husband you could have wished for. He was a real saint.

We never, ever had an argument. She was the most perfect person in the world.

ADJUSTMENT

I'm looking forward to doing things again. I'm making plans.

I have more good days than bad ones now.

That knot in my stomach has gone.

I can look back at what happened and it doesn't get to me like it used to.

Why me? I guess I've learned that these things don't just happen to other people – they happen to ordinary people like me too.

I know I can survive this.

I'm not embarrassed about crying anymore, I let myself have my feelings.

I have so much more strength inside me than I knew was possible.

I am more sensitive to other people going through their tough times. I have learned a lot.

I have a new outlook on life, a new appreciation.

I remember being told of my brother's death by two police officers like it happened yesterday. I became very robotic and stepped into the practical role of bringing my family together to share the news. Identifying his body with my mum was part of this day. My sister was living in Bendigo and Dad was interstate with work, it was not until late that night that we were all together. My granddad and I drove to Bendigo to tell my sister who flatly refused to hear or believe that he was dead and kept saying she only spoke with him the other day.

Arranging the funeral kind of kept me together and busy. It wasn't until sometime after that the reality of his loss sunk in. When you realise there are no more of his dirty socks under the couch or episodes of his favourite TV show to watch with him.

It's funny how grief catches you in unexpected ways. Like when I had my daughter and realised she would not know her uncle and worse he would not know her. It was like I still had regrets years later, wishing that there had been a way to get him through those tough teenage years. I'd give anything to have an adult brother. I have so much space, time and love for him yet he is never coming back.

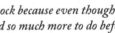

I went numb … I think I went into shock because even though I knew it could happen this wasn't the time and we had so much more to do before the time … I actually went outside and screamed "NO!" so many times I think anyone around thought I had lost my marbles , but I couldn't actually see anyone … I rang work and said to my boss at the time, Glen has gone and I won't be back … In the afternoon I went for what started as a walk then ran and ran and ran and fell down and cried myself silly and remember my sister picking me up and taking me home.

OMG was I a mess … because I wasn't ready for it, and you know, you never are.

Another myth about grief is linked to the time it takes to adapt to your new life. While grief might begin with thoughts like: *Tell me it's not true … It seems like it's all a bad dream*, it may take many days, or even weeks to realise just what's happened. But when the numb-like feelings of shock and disbelief wear off, the agony of the truth must be lived, the aloneness must be endured and the pain of grieving really begins.

Oh, I also remember people telling me time heals and it will get better. This pissed me off as I had no idea what their time frame was, all I knew was that I felt physically sick and heavy with sadness. I wanted to feel better, move on etc. but I felt anchored and trapped by the sorrow ... people referring to time seemed so trivial and impossible. What did they mean — a week, month, year?

There often comes a time that people, who have been so helpful initially, are no longer around. Their lives, while saddened by the event, are not changed, damaged, turned upside down, torn apart, disillusioned and empty. While friends, neighbours, workmates and the rest of the world resume normal living, for the bereaved, the months ahead, and even those first few years, are like mini battlefields – whichever way they look there's a problem advancing.

Memories are a problem. They're glad they have them but sometimes they just keep getting in the way. Conversation is a problem. Who's interested in talking about the weather or the football scores right at this point in time? Sleeping is a problem and night time can be an enemy – all those silent hours to magnify the loneliness. Cooking, working, making decisions, socialising and almost every ordinary task of living can suddenly present itself as a problem. All of this is made worse in a society that doesn't seem to understand.

And here's the dilemma for the bereaved and those around them. When you're grieving, your ability to think clearly and solve your problems tend to disappear under the weight of your grief. Even if you knew where to turn, there's no energy to mobilise yourself and possibly no desire either – *"What's the use now? I've got no reason to go on living."*

While all this is going on for the bereaved, the dilemma for friends is to stand by, powerless, as they *watch* the pain, *see* the confusion and *hear* the "if onlys". In their desire to be helpful, some people try to hurry their grieving friend along, urging them not to look backwards or inwards or in any direction other than forwards, towards the future. Whilst such advice is given with genuine concern, grief is not something that can be avoided or rushed because it makes others uncomfortable. In addition, grief is heavily preoccupied with examining the past and the present in order to make adjustments for the future.

Remember the jigsaw – your grieving friend is going to examine every piece of his or her puzzle and mull over how it's all going to fit back together. It's going to take a long time to work this out and that's how long grief will last. You see, I haven't put a date or time frame to it because everyone is going to tackle their rebuilding project differently. But I can say this – I am not surprised to find many people still struggling to build their new life after just one year and many people I know have taken two, three, four and many, many more years to do so.

If you truly want to help, your words and actions must be aimed at allowing this kind of grief to surface and anything or anyone that tries to block this is acting as a hindrance rather than a helper. You must be aware that to move from the first day of hearing the news that a tragedy has happened to reaching a point where you feel able to cope with the adjustments you've had to make, requires time, patience, stamina, determination, flexibility and hope – both for the bereaved and the helper. But it's not impossible to get there.

CHAPTER 2

AT A GLANCE

- Grieving is about the natural response we have to all types of life crises. It will be expressed in the way we think, feel, behave and our health and general wellness are usually also affected.

- Try not to classify grief into a time-tabled series of responses because this will not help you to understand what is unique about your friend's grief.

- When someone dies, the survivor's grief will be affected by many variables. There's no pattern to follow. There's no 'one size fits all', even in the same family.

- Some grief reactions are expected – sadness, loneliness, anger, confusion and the like. But also allow talk of bitterness, jealousy, disappointment at God, fury at the world, fears for one's sanity, feeling the presence of a loved one in the house and more. Most of these will pass and are all part of the struggle to readjust.

CHAPTER 3

WHERE THERE'S LOSS, THERE'S GRIEF

We often reserve the word 'grief' for people coping with the death of a loved one. In reality though, if we look around us, people every day, everywhere, are coping with grief – grief over the loss of someone or something significant in their lives that has been taken from them. Losses like:

- Separation/divorce
- Retrenchment, retirement, loss of job – lost income, routines, self esteem, goals
- Loss of good health, youthfulness, energy
- Relationship/friendship breakdown
- Loss of home and possessions through natural disasters, addictions, financial problems, divorce
- Disability, loss of body part or bodily function, loss of ability to do things for yourself
- Loss of hopes, plans, dreams, lifestyle
- Bankruptcy – loss of dignity, status, self esteem, financial security
- Abortion, miscarriage, infertility
- Being a carer – loss of your time, usual role, freedom, lifestyle, expectations
- Dementia – losing the person we once knew
- Financial loss through gambling, addiction, failed investments
- Loss of homeland through migration, war, resettlement
- Mental illness
- Ageing – loss of mobility, memory, independence, senses, choices, your home ... it's a long list.

The grief that results from loss is real, painful and legitimate. Shock, despair, anger, frustration, fear, guilt, loneliness, sadness, resentment, preoccupied thoughts, issues with sleeping, eating and general wellness. Again, the list is endless.

What this means is that there are people around us every day who could use the kind of help that encompasses good listening and empathetic responses. Sometimes people, who are grieving over a loss which doesn't involve a death, think they have no right to be upset – there are so many worse things that could happen. But it's our role as friends and helpers to let them know their grief is no less legitimate and no less deserving of our genuine interest and care.

Even though we lost our house in the floods, I felt that I shouldn't be so upset. After all, there were people in our community who lost their loved ones, some lost their children. But I struggled to keep my devastation to myself, I just didn't know how we would cope with this, how we would re-build, how we would get back on to our feet. I was overwhelmed with such fear and uncertainty that it was all I would think of every minute of the day. It was like a re-play: the roar of the waters, the frantic phone calls, the panic, fearing for our lives. How was I ever going to get back to normal?

In November 2013, I was diagnosed with breast cancer. Two weeks later, I'd had a lumpectomy which removed two tumours, several pathology tests and a recommendation by my surgeon that I would need radiation therapy to target any stray cancer cells. I thanked my lucky stars that I'd gotten off so lightly.

But at my post operative check up, the diagnosis had changed. The tumours were much larger than anticipated. I needed to begin a treatment of chemotherapy plus radiation.

I was shocked with this news. How could this be happening to me? I'm so fit and well and look a picture of good health – on the outside.

Next I was off to the oncologist – he would be my chemotherapy doctor. A very personable man, he explained I would need to go back to hospital to have a 'portacath' inserted in my chest which would deliver the chemo to my body. I'd be having a third generation chemotherapy known as FEC, followed by something called Taxotere. In plain English, it meant 18 weeks of chemotherapy, a short break, then 6 weeks of radiation followed by 5 years of hormone therapy. One by one he explained the side effects – tiredness, nausea, vomiting, skin changes, risk of infection, constipation, hair loss and more. I'd already read up on chemotherapy and radiation and everything I read said the good news is that hair loss was only a possible side effect and didn't necessarily happen to all chemo patients.

So when it came to question time the first question I asked was what percentage of patients actually lose their hair? Gently, but very truthfully, the oncologist explained that there were many things he could not guarantee about my health but he knew one thing for sure – all patients taking this particular type of chemo will lose their hair. I would lose not just the hair on my head but eyebrows, eyelashes, *all* body hair.

I know I left his office in shock, too shocked to even cry. And so began one of the biggest challenges for me in having cancer – I think I was okay about the cancer, I was confident they'd get it, but I know I wasn't okay about losing my hair.

The first time I noticed my hair had started to fall out, I couldn't think of what to do so I sent this text to my family: *"My hair has started to fall out. I'm at work in a meeting, so I can't even cry."*

So what did hair loss mean to me?

- Loss of my identity – I am a professional career woman, not a bald cancer patient
- Loss of my usual appearance – I just didn't look like me
- Loss of my familiar face – no eyebrows and eyelashes meant no 'face' – I looked blank
- Loss of privacy – once you go out with a turban on your head it screams 'I've got cancer, I've got no hair'
- Loss of control – there was nothing I could do about this.

Once the treatment started there were new losses because of what chemo was now doing to my body and my lifestyle:

- Loss of energy and general wellness
- Loss of job role – I've had to modify my work schedule
- Loss of taste and appetite – everything I put in my mouth tasted awful
- Loss of daily routine – working, morning walks, housework all needed to change

- Loss of memory – nicknamed 'chemo brain', words just wouldn't pop into my head
- Loss of simple pleasures – my morning skinny flat white coffee, my after work glass of wine
- Loss of certainty and security – how was my future going to turn out? Would I be okay?

There is a principle about loss – **losses rarely exist alone** and we need to understand that the original loss usually triggers many more associated losses.

Another loss that many people experience is their disappointment or dismay at what friends say to them. They'll find that some people don't know what to say, so stay away. Others think they have to say something cheery to brighten you up. Others don't know how to mention what's happened and talk about everything else except the issue at hand. Some can't even say the word 'cancer'. And then there are those who want to say something philosophical to help you look on the bright side.

Here are some of the comments made to me when my hair fell out:

- "When your hair grows back it'll be much thicker than before."
- "It'll probably come back all curly."
- "It could have been worse; you could have lost your breast."
- "Think of all the money you'll save on shampoo and the hairdresser."
- "You can get fabulous wigs these days."
- "You have a great shaped head for baldness."

None of these comments made me feel better. Although I understand the motivation behind them, you can't whitewash someone's grief with a snappy answer. I knew my hair would grow back. I knew I was fortunate not to have had a mastectomy. I knew I wouldn't have the expense of regular visits to the hairdresser. But the reality was, I'd give anything not to have been put in this position in the first place. I didn't want curly hair. I didn't want a nice wig. I just wanted my old hair and my old life back. That's the honest truth.

What I would have preferred to hear was something like this:

- "Gosh, it's going to be really hard to get used to having no hair."
- "I can see you're upset at the thought of losing your hair."
- "It looks like you've got a big challenge ahead of you."
- "No hair, that must be awful for you."

When someone's loss isn't recognised, it means they can't grieve openly about it. Maybe they can't talk about it either. This kind of experience is called 'disenfranchised grief' – a concept that was first described by American researcher, Dr Kenneth J. Doka[11], in 1989. He defined disenfranchised grief "as grief that persons experience when they incur a loss that is not or cannot be openly acknowledged, socially sanctioned or publicly mourned".

Your grief can be unrecognised:

- When the **relationship** is not recognised – such as the close ties of friends, a secret lover, same sex couples, foster parents, colleagues, roommates, teenage romance, step parents and step children.

- When the **loss** is not acknowledged – death of an ex-spouse, miscarriage, abortion, having a disabled child, being an adopted child, placing a child up for adoption, pet loss, financial ruin, loss of home/personal possessions, boyfriend/girlfriend relationships, mental illness, loss of hair/physical appearance due to chemotherapy or illness, death of a public figure or personal hero you admired, death that occurs to people you are not personally acquainted with but touches you such as victims of war, natural disasters, crime, capital punishment, misadventure – and more.

- When the **griever** is excluded – thought to be too young, judged as not central to the relationship, overlooked due to culture, mental disability or ageing. It could be the loss of access to grandchildren or extended family because of divorce or conflict.

- When the **circumstance** is taboo – suicide, AIDS, drug overdose, anorexia, addiction.

Here is a tip you can give to someone who is facing disenfranchised grief:

Remind yourself that you are the best expert on your grief. Your loss is real, whether or not other people recognise it. Your grief is what you say it is, because you are the one going through it.

CHAPTER 3

AT A GLANCE

- Loss and grief go hand in hand. We grieve because of death, divorce, unemployment, loss of health, limbs or physical appearance, loss of purpose and self esteem – loss of anyone or anything that matters to us.

- Sometimes grief becomes 'disenfranchised' – it's not acknowledged or accepted and the griever is ignored or not supported. It doesn't help when support and comfort are offered for other losses, that are perceived to be 'acceptable,' but are not as readily on offer to you.

- Sometimes grief can be further disenfranchised by well-meaning family and friends when they set a time limit on your grief or expect you not to cry or encourage you to "move on" or "get over it". This can result in the griever feeling even more lonely, misunderstood and isolated.

CHAPTER 4

SHOULD I BRING UP THE SUBJECT?

So you're worried about 'putting your foot in it' – should you talk about what's happened or stay right away from the subject? Should you wait for them to bring it up first?

I once asked a young widow who I know to suggest what she needed from her friends who visited after her husband's death. "Avoid avoidance", was her reply. I liked that. Instantly I knew what she was talking about – all the words and strategies people use to avoid what's happened, often beginning with the word *dead* itself. There is an almost endless list of euphemisms we can choose from if we wish to replace *that* word:

- gone
- in heaven
- lost
- a star in the sky
- deceased
- gone to eternal life
- at peace
- departed
- sleeping with the Lord
- at rest
- no longer with us

These days, I even hear the well-worn 'passed away' replaced with just the simple word 'passed': "My father passed during the night.". It's so much nicer than saying, "he died"!

And what about animals? They are 'put to sleep' or 'put down' when in fact they D-I-E. There's no doubt that many of these terms sound softer and do not make us flinch like plain D-E-A-D can.

Some expressions we use even make light of the subject, perhaps again to avoid the sombreness of reality:

- six feet under
- snuffed it
- kicked the bucket
- carked it
- pushing up daisies!

But there really is no need to purposely avoid using the word *dead* in an effort to protect others, or even ourselves. Sooner or later the truth has to be faced that someone has actually D-I-E-D.

Attitudes to funerals and viewings, seeing the person who has died, are often clear examples of avoidance behaviour especially in the context of shielding others from even more pain. Whenever we are involved in funeral arrangements, the helper's aim should be to circumvent possible regrets that may arise later and that often can't be foreseen by grieving people. Because we cannot re-do a funeral when everyone is thinking more clearly, the rule is to 'get it right the first time'.

Deep down, I have always been sorry that the girls didn't say good bye to their brother. Now they wish they did too but a nurse at the hospital said it was better to remember him as he was.

I deeply regret not involving my wife in the burial process [of our son]. I felt it was my job to shield her from such unpleasantness. I believe I lost a golden opportunity for us to get really close. I should have given her more credit for her ability to cope. I also regret allowing the doctors to drug her in hospital. Her grieving process was delayed for no good reason other than that a blubbering ex-mother was an inconvenience.

The most profound regret of them all is my own rejection of the presence of family and friends at Tristan's funeral. I explicitly asked them all, through my parents, to stay away from the funeral and not to send flowers. I was so immersed in a stupid desire to shield my grief from them all that I passed up a truly once in a lifetime chance to spill my grief. I have no doubt that a proper funeral rather than the simple grave side service would have purged me and my wife of a lot of grief. As an altar boy in my childhood I had seen the deep grief at children's funerals and I was too proud to let anyone see me in such a condition.

Whispering the name of the person who has died, or completely leaving it out of the conversation, is another example of avoidance:

After our baby died we hung a photograph of her beside that of our older child. These large portraits of our daughters couldn't be missed when you walked into our family room. But you know what happened when people came to visit? They commented on the photo of our three-year-old but not a word was said about our baby.

It's okay to talk about my husband. He has only died. He has not never existed.

There were people who couldn't even acknowledge the fact that Jessie had died or even existed. But the people that openly told us how they felt about Jessie's death were the ones who helped us the most; the ones that could both laugh and cry about the things Jessie had done with them.

On many occasions I have heard a stillborn child referred to as 'it' or 'the baby' rather than by the name he or she was given. In years gone by, parents in such circumstances were not even encouraged to name their child; after all, they were told, your baby didn't really live! It was only in the mid 1980s, through the efforts of bereaved parents, that stillborn children in Australia were legally allowed to be registered at birth and therefore entitled to a birth certificate. Some years after that, a change in legislation meant their names were allowed to be recorded on a government census for the first time.

This lack of recognition of the value of life at infancy stems as much from our society's perception as it does from people who believe that a baby's death is easier to handle than that of an older child or an adult. In fact, parents who are encouraged to minimise the loss of their baby with advice like, *"Don't cry, you're young enough to have more … It would have been worse if you'd brought the baby home"*, may find themselves still mourning the loss years later. Simply because they were not allowed to grieve at the time of the death. Most of us would judge it unthinkable to totally ignore the death of a parent, spouse or best friend, but for years parents of young infants who died were rarely encouraged to see their child or say goodbye.

The hush-hush approach to someone who has died is also evident in the way some people apologise when they let the dead person's name slip out – as if they have caused offence:

Alice: *I was only telling my neighbour the other day about those camping holidays we had with you and Bill and the kids. They were so much fun.*

Maree: *Yes, Bill just loved that spot we had down by the river. Going camping won't be the same any more … (She starts to cry.)*

Alice: *Oh, Maree, I'm so sorry. I shouldn't have talked about Bill. Now I've gone and upset you.*

In this example, we need to be aware that the mention of Bill's name probably wasn't the cause of the tears. Maree is sad because Bill is no longer around. In fact, being allowed to cry and then continue the conversation might just be what Maree needs – a chance to tell someone what it's like to go about her everyday life without someone as special as Bill.

So let's do a re-run of that conversation and use it to help Maree talk about her feelings:

Alice: *I was only telling my neighbour the other day about those camping holidays we had with you and Bill and the kids. They were so much fun.*

Maree: *Yes, Bill just loved that spot we had down by the river. Going camping won't be the same any more … (She starts to cry.)*

Alice: *You're right Maree. We're all going to miss him on holidays this year. I guess you miss him in lots of ways every day.*

Maree: *I sure do. I still can't get used to doing things on my own. You know, sometimes I go to set a place for him at the dinner table and then when I realise that he's not coming home I get upset all over again.*

Alice: *It must be so hard to get used to all those little things ...*

In this way the conversation can continue with Alice and Maree speaking just as they normally would together. Alice need not become tense as she tries to avoid all those words which she thinks are going to set off memory triggers and make Maree cry, while Maree knows that she is free to talk about her feelings because Alice doesn't show signs of feeling uncomfortable. Instead, they can both relax and let the conversation flow.

Another example of avoidance behaviour is simply to dodge the bereaved person – cross the street when you see them coming or change aisles in the supermarket before they see you.

Since the funeral, a number of our friends have told me that they didn't come to the hospital in those last few weeks because they didn't know what to say to him because he was dying. But they could have just come up to talk about all the things they used to talk about. They didn't have to say anything special.

I went back to work a few months after my daughter died. I sensed a real tension whenever I entered the staff room. I would come in one door and slowly people began to filter out the other.

After our little girl died, some people couldn't even look us in the eye. They would scurry off as if we had the plague.

The following poem, written by a widow, talks more about the disappointment caused by elusive friends:

LETTER TO A LOST ONE

It's been eighteen months now since you left,
You know, we had 200 people at your funeral.
Most of them friends, not acquaintances!
I wonder where they have all gone.
Isn't it funny that they are all so busy!
They seemed a while ago to suddenly have so many commitments.
It seems as though you dying left me with a disease!

Maureen McCormack

Avoidance behaviours are often protective measures in disguise. We believe that by keeping silent we are helping to keep all that grief away. However, if we can learn to accept that grief is not something to be feared, we can also learn ways of approaching someone's grief without discomfort or embarrassment or whatever it is that makes us feel awkward. We might even be able to see that our protective actions are not just directed towards others – we may also be trying to protect ourselves.

Here are some of the ways my friends expressed themselves when they heard the news of my cancer. I was overwhelmed by those who made contact by email and spoke up, shared their disbelief, offered encouragement – because I know it's hard to take that first step. Others couldn't even say the "C" word, they said nothing, they stayed away.

How saddened I am to hear that you are experiencing the 'dreaded cancer' in your life.

I cannot begin to understand the feeling of losing your hair, it's always known as our crowning glory ...

I know you will do everything in your power to get well and I believe the healing effects of relaxation and mediation are invaluable and a great source of inner strength ... may you go well.

There are no words but tears in my eyes as I read your thoughts and feelings about what you have been going through.

This morning on checking my emails I found your email and I have to admit I did get a blow to my stomach.

May the healing spirit of the universe be with you every day, may you always be blessed with the strength to keep moving forward every day.

What a shock for you ... challenging times ... I feel for you.

With your permission I will put you on the prayer chain at our church.

I'm no good at these emails but my best of thoughts are with you during these challenging times.

I wish you a speedy recovery and a cold Sav Blanc in the very near future.

We have spent today trying to think of something inspirational to say, sorry seems sort of empty, "That sucks" seems far more appropriate.

We will be praying and cheering for you. I am sure it will take time for this news to sink in for all.

CHAPTER 4

AT A GLANCE

- In an effort to make things a little easier for someone who is grieving, helpers may avoid saying and doing certain things:
  - mentioning the name of the person who has died
  - changing the conversation if it starts to get emotional
  - suggesting ways of "looking on the bright side"

But grief is not lessened by simply avoiding the subject.

- We need to be aware that by protecting people from talk of death or voicing their feelings, we may actually be motivated by a need to protect ourselves.

- When grieving people are encouraged to keep their grief silent, it may result in unresolved feelings and issues which can cause more problems at a later time.

CHAPTER 5

HOW ARE YOU?... AND THEN WHAT DO I SAY?

After saying "Hello", probably the most common greeting we use these days is, *"How are you?"*. Yet, this simple, everyday question can cause a real dilemma for the bereaved. If they meet someone who politely asks, "How are you?", it's often far simpler to say, "Fine thanks" than to explain how things really are. Generally speaking, it's probably become a habit for many of us to say *"fine"* or *"good"* or *"alright"*, even when we're not.

"When people ask me how I am, I know they want me to say I'm fine. But I'm not. Yet I say 'fine thanks' just to keep them happy."

Imagine a friend's response if you replied, *"Well to tell you the truth, I'm just terrible. I cried for hours yesterday and it seems like I'm never going to get over this. I feel like running away so I don't have to face it!"*. Chances are, this friend will think twice about asking how you are the next time you meet.

Yet it can be very stressful for grieving people to constantly mask their exact feelings because they know others feel uncomfortable if they speak the truth. The awkward silence which may follow a *real* answer is often a signal for the bereaved to keep quiet in future.

So, there's a real no-win situation here if you are grieving. If you're honest, people may become uneasy but if you say you're alright they'll go away thinking that you're over it when, in fact, you're not.

If you genuinely want to know how a grieving person is getting along, there is a handy communication tool which lets them know they can be frank with you. It's called the 'second chance' question and it works like this:

James: Hi Sam, how are you?
Sam: I'm fine thanks.

James: *Oh? (a little puzzled). I noticed yesterday you were so quiet at the office break up. Everything really alright with you?*

Sam: *Well, to tell the truth, since Sue left me I just don't feel like socialising. Watching everyone having a good time there yesterday just got to me. I just wanted to get the hell out of there!*

By asking the question again, with a change of wording or a different emphasis, James has given his workmate a second chance to answer the question in the way he really wanted to – with honesty. When you do the same for a grieving friend, there is a bonus as well. You give them an opportunity to off-load some of their feelings, as your question invites them to share their burden with you – but only if they wish. They are not being forced to divulge anything that may be too personal; they can still respond to your second question by saying, "I really am okay. Please don't worry about me."

Some other second chances can be worded like this:

Sarah: *Hello Chris, how are you?*
Chris: *Oh … I'm okay I guess.*
Sarah: *Okay? You sound a bit hesitant. Is everything alright?*

Joe: *How are you doing mate?*
Mike: *You know, not bad … not bad.*
Joe: *Sounds to me like you aren't too good either. Now how are things really going at home?*

Alan: *Hi Jenny, how are things with you?*
Jenny: *All right I suppose.*
Alan: *Just all right? Tell me what that really means.*

Some questions the bereaved are asked may be too direct and can sound abrupt, even thoughtless:

Are you still upset about your father's death?
Have you accepted it yet?
Are you still grieving?
Are you coping?
Are you over it yet?

Such questions are not simple to answer. Although they may just require a quick "yes" or "no" they don't necessarily give the full story. For the bereaved, "getting over it" may not be so clear cut. Some days may be easier to cope with than others. Some feelings may have lessened but others could still be intense and hard to handle. And what does coping really mean – that I shouldn't still be upset? That I've got my act together and stopped crying?

Questions which illicit a *"yes"*, *"no"* or one word answer are called 'close-ended' because they don't encourage the speaker to give much information and consequently the conversation can easily come to a standstill. If you want to give someone a real opportunity to do some talking, then try an open-ended question – one that provides a chance for lots of details or disclosure:

How are things with you these days?

What's been happening since I last saw you?

Tell me about the kids … How are they doing?

How are you coping on your own now?

Questions like this let the bereaved have their say. They can still give a short answer if they wish, but there is plenty of scope to say much more.

The same happens when you make an enquiry like this:

I often wonder how you're really getting on. You look okay when I see you at work but I'm not sure we're seeing the real you. Am I right?

I haven't seen you at the last two meetings. I guess it's not easy coming along by yourself …

These statements are designed to get the bereaved to fill you in. They are given a lead and you let them follow it through. Again, if they don't feel like talking they can simply say, "Don't worry. Everything's fine." But if it's not, your question has shown that you are sensitive to their loss. This also helps the bereaved to know that they are not as isolated in their grief as they might think.

There is an underlying benefit behind these questions as well. They actually indicate to the bereaved that it is all right to talk about what happened and how they feel about it because you have asked in such a way that they know they don't have to pretend or even protect you from what may very well be a sad, bitter or angry response. Grieving people often welcome this kind of latitude – they can just be themselves and tell their story like it really is.

By asking questions which are designed to get the real story, you also don't fall into the trap of telling the bereaved how they *should* be feeling. Nor will you act like some well-wishers who try to console by telling them about someone who is worse off than they are:

Just think of those parents who lose an only child. That would be much worse. At least you've got the other two.

You're better off than my cousin. She was only 46 when her husband died. At least your Jim was around long enough to see his grandchildren.

You're lucky he went quickly dear. You didn't have to watch him suffer like I did with my husband and his dementia.

Whilst comments like these are intended to reduce the grief, often the opposite actually occurs. It is infuriating, confusing, even depressing to find that no one seems to understand how your situation really is – to hear about somebody else's misfortune certainly does not alter your own. A widow explains:

Don't tell me about other tragedies like someone's child who was killed or died. Is that supposed to make my loss bearable?

One of the most effective ways I have learned to ask, *"How are you?"*, is to say something like: *"How are things going at your place these days?"*. I find this question is so open that it invites a variety of responses either about yourself or other members of the family.

Let's look at how a conversation opener like this could work:

Kate: Hi Sue, how are things going at your place these days?

Sue: So so, I guess. The kids are a bit of a handful on my own and they keep asking about their dad.

Kate: I guess that's a really hard one to answer.

Sue: It sure is. And then there's all that legal stuff – it's the last thing I need right now. Then to top it off the car broke down on me yesterday and I just burst into tears right in the middle of all the traffic. Sometimes I feel like I'm going crazy.

Kate: You've got so much on your plate at the moment, no wonder you end up in tears.

Sue: Gee, I seem to do a lot of crying …

Kate: You've got a lot to cry about when you think of all those years you and Tony were together and what about all those plans you still had?

Sue: Yes, I so regret that we never got to those retirement years that we used to dream about …

This conversation could go on at length with Sue free to talk as much as she likes without the subject being changed, especially when she starts to cry. People like Sue must be able to sense that their friend is comfortable with whatever response is made and that their frankness does not cause others to withdraw. Under such conditions, communication is made easy, even when the subject is a difficult one.

Let's go back to the conversation with Sue. What if Sue avoided all talk about how she was managing at the moment which, after all, is what I really want to know about? I could listen to her telling me about the kids, the legal problems, the car and anything else. To get her to focus on herself, after a while I could simply say something like: *"And what about you Sue, how are you coping with all this?"* I am amazed at the number of times this question has been followed with a *"Do you really want to know?"* response. I guess so many grieving people are used to their friends not wanting to know that they are a little surprised when they are invited to talk about what's happened *and* how they feel about it.

So use questions to help the grieving person talk about how things really are. Once they are at ease with you, you can keep the conversation on the subject by using additional enquiries like:

And how did that make you feel?

And what did you do next?

How would you prefer people to treat you?

I'm not sure I'm getting the picture. Can you explain what you mean by that?

But if you do ask you must be prepared to listen to the answer, and listening is one of the most critical skills of someone who wants to help.

Now – to my favourite question. This is just a simple technique but it is an effective conversation opener and one that is useful in any situation. I'm often asked how you get a conversation started when someone is going through a bad time. How do you bring up the subject? This is how I do it – you simply have to ask what happened.

I just heard about your Dad – do you mind if I ask what happened?

I didn't even realise your Mum was so sick. Can I ask what happened?

I just found out about Michael's accident. It's such a shock. Is it okay if I ask what happened?

What an awful thing for you to go through. Can you tell me what happened?

I can't believe what you're telling me – your baby was stillborn. Is it OK if I ask what happened?

It's simple. To the point. Conversational. Natural. And gives the grieving person permission to tell their story.

CHAPTER 5

AT A GLANCE

- The question, *"How are you?"* could be a difficult one to answer when you're grieving because you might not be sure if your friend is prepared for the real answer or whether a neutral reply like *"Fine thanks"* is what they're hoping to hear.

- There are a number of enquiry techniques which allow you to find out how a grieving person is really coping. Sometimes you may need to ask the same question in a different way to let your friend know you are giving them a chance to talk about their feelings if they want to. A key word here is *latitude* – ask questions that give scope for honest answers.

- Remember two simple conversation openers are:

"How are things going at home these days?"

"Is it OK if I ask what happened?"

CHAPTER 6

LISTENING FIRST, THEN EMPATHY

If you ask the bereaved what they want most from the people around them, one comment is rarely left off their list – "just someone who'll listen".

I need to be listened to, to know that I'm okay. I've found, however, that I have to be very selective in who I choose to speak to. They all think I'm over it, but this clever charade is only because I've found so few people able to listen.

No one would talk to me about her. They had this wrong idea that they shouldn't upset me, so don't talk about it. I called myself "the man in the bubble". A couple of times I tried to bring it up with other people, they just couldn't handle it. They changed the subject, looked at their feet, looked at the ceiling.

Listening to grieving people is not a passive business. Whilst it seems elementary, it can be one of the most difficult of all helping skills. Good listening is far from easy and you need to be good at it if you want to be good at responding with empathy. It requires you to be actively engaged with the feelings of the other person. To do that effectively takes concentration and self discipline and it only works when there is a genuine desire to help.

What's so special about listening? How does it work? First and foremost, when we listen to someone with a problem, it allows them to talk freely about a matter of real importance to them. In being allowed to talk openly, the problem is aired and examined, thoughts are clarified and possibly decisions can then be made and action taken. When you are expected to clam up that's just where your problem stays – locked up tight, right along with all the feelings you have about it and we've already seen evidence of what can happen when you can't get your feelings out.

In her book *The Rules Of Inheritance,* American author Claire Bidwell Smith[12], describes the experience of losing both her parents by the time she was in her twenties. She struggled to work out how to manage being an adult orphan and to find people who understood how this had affected her, especially the intense isolation of having no-one to talk to. She explains it like this:

There's something incredibly lonely about grieving. It's like living in a country where no one speaks the same language as you. When you come across someone who does, you feel as though you could talk for hours.

Listening to grieving people allows them to do something else – to verbalise their list of all the things that mattered in the relationship which has now ended. Every grieving person I have ever known has had such a list, crammed with details which outsiders could never have known, but which recorded the significance of the past as well as future plans and hopes and dreams. The list, by the way, may not be written in black and white but make no mistake it's there. And it only needs some words like, "Tell me about …" to start the story rolling.

This reminds me of a headstone I once saw commemorating the life and untimely death of a much loved daughter. It was completed with a variation of Elizabeth Browning's famous words: *How much did we love her? Let us count the ways …* When we listen to a grieving friend, we let them do their 'counting'. This usually means the bereaved will want to retell their story over and over. While outsiders may become irritated and even bored with hearing the same old details, for the bereaved it helps to bring their loss out into the open and make real a seemingly impossible event. Eventually, the story will lose its prominence in their lives as the bereaved allow new things to enter.

Thich Nhat Hanh calls it 'compassionate listening' – *You listen with only one purpose: to help him or her to empty his heart. You just listen with compassion and help him to suffer less. One hour like that can bring transformation and healing.*

Here are some tips for compassionate listening:

1. Look like you are listening.

Make sure your body language conveys an interest in what is being said. If you lean slightly towards a person, they perceive this gesture as a sign of interest whilst tightly folded arms or constant glances at a watch or passers by, may be interpreted as disinterest, impatience or discomfort with what is being said. Even where you sit can make a difference – talking to someone from behind your desk or across a table may not be as easy as if you pulled up a chair beside them.

2. Sound like you are listening.

Keep the conversation flowing. A well placed "uh-huh" is as good as saying "I can see what you're getting at" without excessive use of words which interrupt the speaker. The words, "Mmmmm", "Oh" and a head nod or two work in just the same way.

If you need some clarification, try using this technique:

Speaker: I'm convinced I'm going crazy.

Listener: Crazy?

Speaker: You know, not sleeping, day dreaming all the time. It's not like me.

By just repeating the last word or two with an enquiring tone, the speaker knows you want some more details but the minimal amount of talking on your part helps to keep the conversation on track.

3. Know whether you are naturally a talker or a listener.

This is where the discipline comes into it. Talkers may find it difficult to keep their enthusiasm for speaking under control. Avoid jumping in with statements like:

The same thing happened to me ...

That reminds me of ...

Did I tell you about the time when ...

Your story can be enough of a diversion for the speaker to put the lid on theirs. Even if you get back to the point by asking something like, *"Now what were you saying?"*, the speaker may have already concluded that you weren't all that interested and close the subject with the reply, *"Don't worry, it wasn't all that important."*

The oft quoted remark on listening is worth repeating again here – *You have two ears and one mouth. Use them in that proportion.*

4. Sit in silence.

It's not unusual for grieving people to require periods of silence while they speak. This may be their way of focusing their thoughts or re-thinking something they have said. To re-tell a critical experience – how it happened, who broke the news, how you reacted, what you saw, said or did and so on is exhausting and emotional. Silence may be necessary as a wind down as well as time to gather some strength. Perhaps a quiet time means your grieving friend still needs to let it all sink in.

You needn't fill these gaps in the conversation. Just by being there you're already doing something helpful – you're sharing their grief.

5. Be comfortable with tears.

There's nothing like someone's tears to make others feel embarrassed and not know where to look or what to say. Often with the best of intentions, we want to say or do something to stop the crying. We want to make it better. But crying is healthy and helpful to your wellbeing. Crying is our body's way of getting rid of toxins and our tears act as a release valve for stress, tension, depression and grief.

So, if someone starts to cry while they are talking to us, we don't need to 'do something' like get them a glass of water or a cup of tea or find them some tissues – just sit with them, stay there, maybe put your arm around them or hold their hand.

If you want to say something, just affirm that you understand why they are crying – "You miss him/her so much". They will stop crying when they are ready. Remember we call it a "good cry" because it's good for us.

Consider the meaning of these statements – they are very permission-giving for tears and sadness:

Ever had a memory that sneaks out of your eyes, and rolls down your cheek ...?

People cry, not because they're weak. It's because they've been strong for too long.

6. Indicate verbally that you understand.

When it's your turn to talk, reflect what you have heard, using your own words. This assures the speaker that you have understood accurately.

Speaker: *It's awful being alone. I can't believe how big this house seems now there's no one to share it.*

Listener: *It sounds like Tom's left a big gap – not just in the house but in your life too.*

Don't be tempted to use exactly the same words as theirs because you will end up sounding like a parrot. Be confident enough to use your own kind of expressions as long as they convey the message precisely.

Mother: *I hate it when it rains at night. All I can think about is my little boy out there in the cold cemetery. That's one of the worst feelings I get. I just want to cuddle him and keep him safe but all I can do is sit here ... all helpless.*

Friend: *That sounds like such an awful thing to live with. It must be so hard not to be able to do all the things you want to do as a Mum.*

As a good listener you need to keep in mind that you are not responsible for fixing, changing, curing or eliminating the pain associated with the story you are being told. Therefore, you need not struggle to find expressions which will presumably do so. Here, I'm referring particularly to all those clichés that are offered to the bereaved as words of comfort. In reality, they offer no sign of understanding – and being understood is one of the most important needs of grieving people.

When my brother died in a boating accident, people kept saying, 'At least he died doing what he loved best'. All I could think about was that he should have been alive and still doing what he loved.

"Oh, you're so strong. You'll be okay." What the bloody hell is that supposed to mean? That I won't, or shouldn't, feel suicidal, shredded, insane, lost, lonely, angry, bitter, hurt, confused, crazy ... Three different people said that to me. It really mystified and hurt me.

A survey[13] conducted by health professionals asked bereaved parents to comment on "unfortunate" statements made to them by others. Here are some of them:

Don't cry, be strong.

I know how you feel.

You should be over the death by now.

Get on with the future, there are others worse off.

It's probably for the best.

These things happen.

You're not the only one.

God has a plan.

Have another baby.

You've changed.

Don't be upset, don't cry.

Life must go on.

More recently, followers of a grief blog were asked to share their comments about the things that were said to them that caused irritation or more hurt. Here are some of them.

I hate when people tell me how strong I am, especially when they follow it up with "I think I would just die if it happened to me". But my least favourite is, "You have to remember you have other children". Like I forgot or they take the place of the child I lost. Mira

As for the "He's in a better place now" or "It was God's will" ... the person in grief needs to reach a point emotionally when they can accept them on their own ... it took me five years ... There are some things we just need to work out for ourselves. Chelsea

My 7-year-old died 31 years ago and I still get this and yes it still hurts! So VERY many people said "you'll have more children", but I wasn't that lucky. Besides it wouldn't have changed how much I loved and still love her! How could she be in a better place, she doesn't have her Mum! And no I will never get over it, time does not heal all wounds and God may have wanted her, but I needed her! Judy

These one-liners are often termed 'grief clichés'. To be honest they are unhelpful clichés. Whilst these statements give you something to say, they probably do little to actually succeed in your intention of wanting to help your friend. On the contrary, they probably tell your friend that you don't understand and that is precisely what you need to avoid. Such statements are really a form of censorship – they try to cover up the true impact of grief by suggesting the bereaved should hurt less, cry less, question less.

Possibly the one statement, in the above list, that causes more grief to the bereaved than any other is, *"I know how you feel"*. This apparently harmless comment has the potential to enrage the bereaved to the point that I hear it mentioned time and time again in this context –

"If one more person says that to me I'm going to scream!"

By saying *"I know how you feel"*, you imply that you shared exactly the same relationship with the person who died as did your grieving friend. This just isn't the case. How can you presume to feel exactly what another person is feeling? If we look at the death of a child in a family as an example, each parent will grieve over different aspects of the relationship which are now lost, as will brothers and sisters. All will have an inventory of what mattered, coloured by their own perceptions, with different conversations to remember, different highlights, different wishes. So the grief will also be different.

Probably the most remarkable come-back I have heard from a widow in response to this unhelpful cliché went like this:

Friend: I know just how you feel.

Widow: Oh, do you? Did you know my husband THAT well!

Let's say you do know what it's like to be widowed, you still don't know what your friend's grief feels like. You only know your own feelings. Let's say you know what it's like to lose a grandparent, mother, father, child, brother or sister. Remember that's your experience of grief. You only know how you felt at the time. It is not the universal grief story.

I'm sure your loss can help you understand situations and problems that bereaved people share – what do you do when that first Christmas comes around? What do you do with all those clothes in the wardrobe? How do you get the courage to start socialising again? What do you say when people ask how many children you've got? Even though these are common dilemmas for the bereaved, they still deserve to be heard in the context of their own unique, personal experience.

CHAPTER 6

AT A GLANCE

Listening is:

- A priceless gift. To listen to a person until that person feels fully heard and knows it, gives value to that person and the experience he wants to tell you about.

- Visible in your body, gestures and eye contact.

- An activity which looks easy on the outside however it is not effortless but rather, it is effortful.

- An opportunity for your friend to "count the ways" he or she remembers the person who died.

- Being comfortable with silence.

- Helping.

Listening is not:

- Giving your advice.

- One liners and clichés.

- Changing the subject.

- Minimising the event – *it could have been worse.*

- Telling your story or the stories of others.

- Fixing the hurt or curing the grief.

CHAPTER 7

WHAT EXACTLY IS EMPATHY?

Listening is important. But grieving people will judge the quality of your listening by your response. So responding effectively is even more important. We do this with empathy. Let's start by talking about sympathy and empathy. Sometimes the two get confused. Sympathy often sounds like this:

I'm sorry for your loss.
I'm sorry to hear about that.
I'm so sorry.

Put simply, being sympathetic, is a way for me to acknowledge your loss. We call it 'giving our condolences'. But it isn't a way of showing that I understand what your loss means to you. I don't need to really know anything about your loss, I can offer my condolences without asking you what happened or how you feel about it.

Empathy, on the other hand, requires more of me, the listener. I need to:

- Invite you to tell your story
- Listen to your inventory – all the bits and pieces, not just the parts about happy memories
- Hear what matters most to you
- Understand what the loss means to you
- Give you permission to have your grief
- Suspend my judgement about your way of handling your grief
- Use words that show I'm on your wavelength
- Leave you in no doubt that I accept and understand your grief
  - that's how it is for you.

Grieving people know when they get empathy and when they don't. And they know how it feels when others have no idea what they are going through – when they don't listen, don't ask or make assumptions about them. Here's an example:

A peer said to me, *"You are back to work too soon." Nothing else like "Good Morning" or "Hello", even a "Hi, how are you?" would have been more sensitive than that and she just walked away. I was gobsmacked and thought what a bitch.*

Another person in the business said to me, "Why would you come back so soon?" (Wow did I feel like shit …) I felt that maybe I didn't actually love Glen and then I just walked out and burst into tears.

Another friend (yes, I still speak to her) said at least you had time to prepare and you knew about Glen's cancer. OMG I thought, how does anyone prepare for death, and why would one of my friends even say that to me?

Then there were the ones that said to me, "You'll get over it, he's in a better place now." (How would they bloody know … have they been there and back?)

Most people obviously thought they were helping me and still today I get, "So have you got somebody new?"… ARGGGGGG I want to say it's only 21 months since I lost Glen, but I don't.

I actually feel sorry for those people because when it happens to them, they may understand! And how bad will they feel.

My brother Steve committed suicide only a few years after I'd had treatment for ovarian cancer. The number of people who made comparisons between my illness and his death was unbelievable. Remarks like, "It must be hard that you fought for your life and he threw his away" really shocked and infuriated me. I was already feeling helpless that I couldn't be the difference he needed in his life not to make that fatal decision and the overwhelming sense of the injustice was all-consuming. My illness was treatable, accepted and supported. When Steve was in hospital there were minimal visitors, no flowers, cards or balloons just more helplessness – such a stark contrast to my hospital and cancer experience.

What if you hear statements like this:

I'm a hopeless father ... If only I'd seen how depressed he was he might still be here.

I'll never get over it ... I'll never be happy again. We were together for more than fifty years.

I can't bear the thought of Christmas coming up. It just won't be the same ever again.

Listening to talk like this can be very hard. The words are raw with pain and point right to the heart of someone's despair. It seems our instincts want to immediately shout, *Don't talk like that! No, you're wrong. You can't blame yourself. You can't throw away the rest of your life because of this. You must try to keep going. You must!* In fact, such conversations have reached a crossroad and the response of the helper is critical.

As a helper, you can respond in a number of ways. Possibly the easiest route if you're feeling uncomfortable is to retreat and make what I call an 'Exit Response'. This can be done physically just by adding a little distance between you and the speaker – shifting in your chair, taking a step or two backwards or leaning away. Other non-verbal signals will also act as clues about your feelings like broken eye contact, fidgeting or sudden glances at your watch. Observing this may be enough of a hint to let your friend know that it's best to drop the subject.

Another 'exit' is to try to reason with your friend. Point out their lack of logic. Tell them they're not thinking straight:

Talking like that is nonsense. Of course you've got plenty to live for. You want to see your kids grow up and have their own families, don't you?

There you go again – always looking at the negative side of things. You're young, you'll get married again.

It's worth remembering that no-one's grief goes away because we tell them not to have it – all it does is shut it down and keep it hidden when it makes others feel uncomfortable. This may lead you to another option where you ask the bereaved to look at it from another point of view – yours:

If I were you I'd be going on a holiday. You need something to look forward to.

If it were up to me I'd have another baby straight away.

If I were in your position I'd sell the house and get away from all those memories.

Or you can make a verbal 'exit' by changing the subject, preferably to something more cheerful:

You're starting to get all morbid. Why don't we talk about something like …

All you do lately is talk about the past. Think of the future …

Enough of all that sad talk. What else have you been up to lately?

Finally, you can respond by being firm – it's time they stopped all this selfish talk and got on with their lives:

You're just feeling sorry for yourself. It's time you pulled yourself together.

I know it's hard, but there are other people worse off than you.

There's no use crying about it. You need to put it behind you and make a fresh start.

Or you can approach the crossroad with a powerful communication tool. Empathy. Remember, don't confuse empathy with sympathy – it's not about saying you're sorry. Empathy is about listening with your heart so that you can tell your friend that you understand what is happening to them.

More importantly, empathetic statements have underlying messages which say you accept where the other person is coming from, even if you have not been there yourself or even if you think you would handle the situation differently.

Empathy always conveys that you see the other person's point of view – it has nothing to do with *your* opinion, advice or beliefs. The power of empathy results from its ability to keep communication open because it does not judge, try to change or solve, belittle or criticise.

When good listening and empathy are combined they are like dynamite – they can help to release built up grief. How? Basically because they allow the grieving person to talk about what's bothering them. This is in direct contrast to what most other people are suggesting – *Don't talk about it. Don't think about what happened. Don't dwell on the past.* This is often termed 'giving permission' and grieving people need to hear out loud that it's all right to do two things: *to talk and to feel.*

When you allow a grieving person to talk, talk and talk you actually allow them to itemise all the aspects of the person and their relationship with him or her that mattered. You see, often you don't fully realise what matters until it's taken away from you. But often the people around you believe it's their role to do the opposite – to tell you that your loss really isn't as bad as you're imagining:

You're lucky, at least he didn't suffer.

You're lucky, you're still young enough to get married again.

You're lucky, at least you didn't go full term.

You'll be surprised how often people are told they are "lucky" when something goes wrong in their lives! So rather than minimise, learn to empathise. This is how it works:

Jane: *I've nothing left to live for. My boy meant everything to me. He didn't deserve to die like this. Why my son? Why our family?*

Allan: *Tim was so special to you, wasn't he? And now you feel life is empty and unfair because he's not here.*

Let's look at Allan's response. There is no 'exit' statement. No advice. No cliché like *"It's God's will"*. No criticism of Jane's feelings. No hidden message telling her she should stop feeling sorry for herself. Instead, Allan lets her know, loudly and clearly, that he has heard her point of view. Even though he may disagree with her conclusion that there is nothing to live for, at this stage he knows she will only trust him with her feelings if he is able to show he understands them. So here, empathy is used to build trust and rapport. Allan knows that the more he does this, the more she is likely to share feelings rather than keep them locked up inside where they won't be dealt with anyway. At the crossroad, Allan has chosen empathy rather than advice because he knows that at this point in Jane's grief, she needs to be heard and advice-giving might just be the cue that prompts her to believe that no one really understands her. If this were to happen, their friendship could begin to break down.

To make empathy even more effective, you must also express your words so that they accurately identify with the tone of the message you have just heard. Imagine someone describing an argument saying, *"He called me every name under the sun and so I yelled back that he had no right to talk to me like that. Boy, was I furious!"* If you were to respond by saying, *"It sounds like you got cross"* your friend would probably be quick to interject saying, *"Cross? I was more than that. I was ready to punch him."* The more precise you are in picking up what your friend is feeling, the more you will show that you have listened well. There is, therefore, a strong link between listening and empathy – if you don't listen well enough, you won't know how to phrase your response and your empathy may be wrongly directed and not as convincing.

Being skilled in the use of empathy requires practice. This means we need to become familiar with it in our everyday conversations and this is often easier than it seems. Look for opportunities in your conversations at work or at home where you can show the other person that you can see things from their point of view. Remember, when you listen and empathise, you are really saying, *Hey that really matters to you, doesn't it. I can see how that's affecting you.*

When we are aware of empathy, there are countless situations where it can be used:

Customer: I'm so upset. I saved for months to buy this and when I got home it broke the first time I used it.

Salesperson: No wonder you're angry. You waited so long to buy this and then our product didn't live up to your expectations.

Teenager: I didn't want to play in that stupid grand final anyway. The coach always picks his favourites.

Parent: It sounds like you're feeling really disappointed because you've been left out of the squad.

Husband: What does a bloke have to do to get ahead? My sales are up, I've brought in new clients, I never take a day off ... and I never get so much as a "thank you".

Wife: I can see how frustrating it is when no-one seems to appreciate your efforts at work.

In all of these circumstances, the conversation could easily continue and allow the speakers to get their feelings off their chest. The listener probably can't change what's happened or make everything right but he can create an atmosphere which communicates: *I can hear that you are upset. I'll keep listening if you want to talk about it some more.*

If you're not sure how to phrase an empathetic statement, you can start with words like:

It sounds like ...

You're feeling ... because ...

It seems there's a lot of (pain/anger/disappointment) in your life because ...

Do be careful, however, not to sound mechanical or unnatural in your response. To me, it is more authentic to speak to a good friend in the language that you use every day rather than risk sounding insincere by using expressions which just aren't like you:

Rob: *I can't believe there's a God in this world. First I lose my eldest in that bike accident and now my other boy's on drugs. What's a father supposed to do?*

Ted: *Things are really tough at your place. It's just not fair.*

Ted's comment has zeroed right in on Rob's despair. He has accurately pitched the level of his empathy, without trying to find fancy or clever words. He had the choice of moralising, advising or saying something to try and snap Rob out of it but at the crossroad he chose empathy as a way of letting Rob know he understands why he's in such despair.

Megan: *Is everything okay with you Sophie? Look at the bags under your eyes.*

Sophie: *I just can't get to sleep. You know, night time's the worst. I lie awake and really think I can hear Tim moving around the house. I know it's wishful thinking but I'd do anything for him to come back.*

Megan: *It sounds like you get really lonely at night. You must be missing Tim like crazy.*

By listening, Megan is saying: *It's alright to tell me what matters to you right now.* Then, by responding with empathy, she is further able to get the message across to Sophie that her loneliness was heard. By staying with the feelings, Megan is creating an outcome for Sophie where she will probably feel better – not because her grief has been taken away, but because some of it has been shared, heard and recognised.

Using empathy in our communication comes down to this. If someone is disclosing something meaningful to us, we've got four broad categories of responses to choose from: *Clichés. Facts. Opinions. Feelings.*

Whether you know it or not, if we were to analyse any conversation, the content would basically be made up of these four components. When we don't know someone well, we often speak more in clichés and facts, like small talk, and as we get to know them better and we've built trust and rapport we are more likely to share opinions. Talking about feelings is often the hardest topic to discuss and for many of us we only do it with a select few people in our lives.

When someone is telling us about their grief, we need to choose a response which validates their feelings – so we in turn choose feeling words to do this. And it can build rapport very quickly. Empathy means choosing a feeling statement in response to another's feeling statement. It simply conveys, 'We're on the same wavelength' and eliminates instances of 'No one understands me'. It reduces the possibility of feeling isolated or misunderstood – all possibilities if a cliché, fact or opinion is the helper's response to a feeling statement.

Here are some examples:

Julie: I can't believe this sort of thing could happen. Everything was going along so smoothly and then they say they don't need me any more. Yesterday I had a job, today I've got nothing.

Mike: CLICHÉ: These things happen, Julie. You'll survive.

       FACT: Well, unemployment is a part of life these days.

      OPINION: You've got lots of skills, I think you'll find something else before you know it.

      FEELING: What a blow you've had – losing your job with no warning at all. It must have come as a real shock.

❖

Terry: Something's not right with Lisa. Since she had the baby she hardly notices me anymore. And she never wants to go out and do anything like we used to. I don't know what's up and I sure don't know what to do about it.

Jeff: CLICHÉ: *Women! It's hard to figure them out!*

FACT: *Having kids always take some getting used to. You'll cope.*

OPINION: *Why don't you take up golf again? At least that'll get you out of the house a bit.*

FEELING: *Lisa's really got you worried, hasn't she? You two were always so close. It must be hard on you.*

❖

Kate: *I don't know how I'm going to cope with Ben's birthday coming up. All I can think about is last year and that big party. And now all I can do is go to his grave and talk to him there and cry.*

Kelly: CLICHÉ: *Please don't cry. Everything will be all right.*

FACT: *Remember you've got all your great memories. You're so lucky to have them.*

OPINION: *If I were you I'd start dating again. You need a new man in your life.*

FEELING: *Facing his birthday is sure going to be a hard day for you. I guess you feel close to Ben when you sit by his grave.*

When you use empathy in your responses you create understanding – empathy creates a link in your relationship. It heightens trust. When you're grieving, this makes it *safe* to talk about how you feel. You know you are being heard even when you think you are going crazy.

One more point about empathy. Don't confuse it with agreement. By choosing words which show you understand where the other person is coming from, you are not exactly saying you agree with what they're feeling, doing or saying. You're just confirming that you hear how they are handling their emotions and what issues matter to them right now.

Here's an example of how this works. We are going to meet Susan who is telling us about the death of her cherished poodle, Edward[14].

Edward was my 25kg big, black, standard poodle – the love of my life. He drew attention wherever he went, he really was soooo handsome.

The day we found a lump in his neck was a real shock. I took him to the vet immediately, I was due to phone for the results on Xmas Eve but could not bring myself to do it ... I phoned after Xmas ... it was a rampant form of cancer. I couldn't let my precious boy have a painful death so I took the option to have him euthanased. I made an appointment for the following Saturday at 8am. That was the longest week of my life ... looking into his big black eyes and knowing that on Saturday I would no longer have him.

On the Friday night I slept with him, I just wanted it to be the two of us. I held him at the surgery as the vet gave the injection ... when I left I remember letting out a huge animal like howl ...

Imagine Susan were telling you this story. You have been listening intently and now you have to say something in response. We need to make sure our empathy is really empathetic. Here are some suggested ways we could respond to her – decide which ones are clichés, facts, opinions and feelings.

1. Oh, that's terrible, it reminds me of my Labrador who died when I was still at school. He was hit by a car.

2. But he was pretty old wasn't he, you were lucky to have him for a long time.

3. Did you get a new dog after that?

4. It would have been worse if someone in your family actually died.

5. It sounds like Edward meant the world to you, I can tell how much you loved him.

6. At least he went quickly and didn't suffer – you did the right thing.

7. I guess that's what happens when you have a pet, you have to prepare yourself that they won't always be around.

8. You're lucky your vet got to it quickly, sometimes you can end up with thousands of dollars in bills.

9. You and Edward were so close, it must have hurt like crazy.

10. That's why I don't have any pets, you just get too attached.

Check your answers – is your empathy really empathetic?

1. FACT: Oh, that's terrible, it reminds me of my Labrador who died when I was still at school. He was hit by a car.

2. CLICHÉ & FACT: But he was pretty old wasn't he, you were lucky to have him for a long time.

3. FACT: Did you get a new dog after that?

4. OPINION: It would have been worse if someone in your family actually died.

5. FEELING: It sounds like Edward meant the world to you, I can tell how much you loved him.

6. FACT & OPINION: At least he went quickly and didn't suffer – you did the right thing.

7. OPINION: I guess that's what happens when you have a pet, you have to prepare yourself that they won't always be around.

8. OPINION: You're lucky your vet got to it quickly, sometimes you can end up with thousands of dollars in bills.

9. FEELING: You and Edward were so close, it must have hurt like crazy.

10. OPINION: That's why I don't have any pets, you just get too attached.

Empathetic responses pick up on the *essence* of the speaker's message. They show we get the picture of what the speaker means and we are on their wavelength:

- What were they trying to get me to understand?
- What mattered most to them?
- Why are they telling me about this?
- What do they want me to know about their experience?
- Why was this so significant to them?
- How do they feel the about this?

CHAPTER 7

AT A GLANCE

Grieving people know when they get empathy and they know when they don't!

You show your empathy by:

- Staying with your friend's feelings, as raw and painful as they may be

- Accepting how your friend is feeling

- Acknowledging what your friend is feeling

- Hearing what matters most – and your friend will know that you 'get it'

- Giving your friend permission to feel the way she wants to feel – it's safe to share feelings with you

- Leaving your friend in no doubt that you are on their wavelength, you've understood the essence of their story.

CHAPTER 8

WILL FAITH FIX IT?

I once received a telephone call from a teenage girl asking for an appointment to see me because she needed some help in coming to terms with her father's death. "I want to bring something to show you," she added. When we met she produced a small package from her jeans pocket and handed it to me saying, "My aunt gave me these and said they would help me cope with my father's death. But I don't know what to do with them."

She had been given a set of rosary beads. Something she had never seen before. I guess she was bewildered at how an object, much like a necklace, was going to make things better. Whilst these were well known to her Catholic aunt, their purpose, and intended benefit, were lost on her niece.

This young girl's experience illustrates a valuable lesson when we talk about the role of faith in the context of grief. We cannot presume that it is for everyone, especially those who have no prior relationship with a church and its teachings. I am not saying that non-church goers cannot receive comfort from the bible or a clergy person but a religious message will be more valuable when it is presented in a way that is relevant to the needs of the grieving person and makes sense in his or her language and experience.

Listen to this example of a clergyman speaking at a funeral ceremony:

How do we come into the presence of God?

The answer is: just as we are.

We come numbed by tragedy.

We come shocked and shaken by loss.

We come in our pain, in our frustration, disappointed and confused and angry.

We come full of questions ...

I believe it is important that we face how we feel, and that we face facts.

I believe that nothing that we do here is other than honest and true and clean.

First, this means that the tragedy of Paul's death, too young by half, needs to be named as a tragedy – pure and simple.

It is no more God's will that he die with still half a lifetime before him than it is our own.

It is positively blasphemous to suggest otherwise.

These words are about the death of a 43-year-old husband and father. The words impact on our ears with their plain, honest and hard-hitting presentation of the facts: Paul died. A tragedy. Too young. Don't blame God.

There is a three-pronged message here for those present at this funeral, and indeed for anyone who wants to offer a grieving friend some Christian words of comfort. Firstly, there is clear acknowledgement of the enormous sense of loss which surrounds this death: *We come in our pain ... We come full of questions ...* Secondly, there is no attempt to offer testimonials from the bible or elsewhere of another's show of strength or faith in times of adversity: *We come as we are ...* Thirdly, there are no one-liners – *It's God's will. God only takes the best. God works in mysterious ways* – designed to offer easy solutions to make sense of this event.

Instead the clergyman continues:

Indeed, God's heart of love is the first to break, and our Christian hope lies not in a God who waves magic wands but in a God who walks with us through the darkness and who makes the darkness light.

So we do not muddy the plain facts about how Paul died, or try to soften its impact with easy, meaningless or pious words.

There is no "Why?" to be answered beyond the medical answer.

In other words, he is saying that the Christian response to death is to see it for what it is – the result of our humanness – human bodies break down, human drivers cause accidents, human doctors cannot cure everyone. Human beings have heart attacks. We need not "muddy" the truth by suggesting otherwise.

So why have religious clichés become so much a part of our language of condolence? My hunch is that it has almost become an automatic response – one we don't give much thought to – the words almost roll off the tongue too easily: *God's will. God's purpose. God's plan. God only takes the best.*

Maybe it's all we can think of when the unthinkable happens. Perhaps in our efforts to find our own answers to tragedy, we place the onus on God because there just doesn't seem to be any other logical explanation. Or is it that we must hold someone responsible and when we can't lay blame with any human cause then God becomes the scapegoat?

Whatever the reason, such thinking becomes particularly unhelpful when we use it to encourage the bereaved to stop their grieving. To imply that God has given them this cross to bear and they must do so with a minimum of fuss, or a maximum of faith, simply puts more strain on them. For practising Christians it may even create feelings of guilt or self doubt as they try to work out why their faith is not lessening their grief.

Graeme Griffin[15], who was quoted earlier, talks about the one-sidedness of faith which results from denying the full range of human emotions, especially when those emotions are hostile or negative:

We seem to feel that we have to be so nice to God and tell him all the time what a great guy he is and so a whole half of our emotional equipment is taken away from us. What is even worse, our relationship with God is put on a totally false footing when we can only express some of the things we feel to him ... when we focus only on the positive, when we can't get the contradictory feelings we have together – the feelings of love and adoration and the feelings of abandonment and hurt and disappointment – when it all has to be one way, we not only cease to be honest with God but we cease to be able to be really helped by the Church ...

The role of faith is that it gives you hope amidst the desolation of hurt, and prayer allows you to talk out your thoughts with someone who you trust to be really listening. But believing in God is not a solution in itself, a panacea, a carpet under which we are meant to sweep our true feelings. When talk of the resurrection is used to replace talk of emotions then all we are offering is pseudo-religious help.

Similarly, when we try to point out the "blessings" of a death, we may be asking people to consider their loss as minimal because their relative or friend is no longer suffering. Whilst it is a comfort to know there is no more pain, what we *know* intellectually and what we actually *feel* may be two different things. The truth is that faith does not prevent the hurt of grief, nor does it compensate for a widow's lonely bed or a mother's empty cradle or a child's missing parent.

I once heard a priest tell a story about a fellow priest who went to visit a family whose child had died of cot death. On his arrival, the mother opened the door and abused the hell out of him – How could God do this? Why must He make the innocent suffer? Why their little one? The priest stayed, quietly. After the anger subsided, both mother and father cried and cried and still the priest stayed. To them, he represented a God who didn't go off in a huff but would stay and accept them as they were, not trying to change their feelings or their beliefs or the situation. He didn't try to cheer them up or cite spiritual quotations. He simply stayed, choosing to be *with* them, rather than talk *at* them. He obviously understood the mechanics of mourning and didn't try to smother their loss in the "niceness" of pseudo-religious talk like, *"God must have needed another little angel in Heaven"*.

In Christian terms, a friend who wishes to help another, need only recall the biblical story of Lazarus to know there is no need to say, *Be brave* or *Be strong*. Upon the death of his friend Lazarus we are simply told, "Jesus wept". These two simple words alone give permission for us to be real about our feelings. They tell us that we are meant to grieve. It's worth remembering that it's often the words of people, not the Gospel, which discourage grieving – in Matthew Chapter 15 we are told: *Blessed are those who mourn, you shall find comfort.*

Here is an inspiring letter, which illustrates how Christian values, faith and a spiritual message are used to comfort the grieving parents of Michael, who died after two years of facing cancer. The letter comes from a teacher at the school which Michael attended.[16]

Dear Mr & Mrs Grennan,

The death of Michael came as quite a shock to me. Ever since I realised the seriousness of Michael's illness my thoughts were with him. Michael's general attitude to life and death over the past twelve months had been a lesson to many students at Marist Brothers/St Mary's High School in Lismore. They have been following his progress through press and personal reports and a personal letter he wrote to my Religion class in October 1982.

Michael's death was tragic, but to know that students who had no personal experience of him, prayed for him regularly and asked often about his progress, is a sign to me that in his short life, he has really given something to the world.

His life and death has strengthened my Faith. The way he carried his heavy cross is a sign to me that without Christ's help, such crosses would be unbearable. To you his parents and family, I write to thank you for his wholesome short life and the inspiration he was to many students and teachers in Lismore.

In contrast, Michael's mother Lorraine, recalls the following not-so-helpful conversation, also of a religious nature. She shows us how easily unhelpful comments can impact negatively on the bereaved and how easily an insightful comment can be a 'pick-me-up' when you're feeling down and deflated.[17]

We have two more funerals to go to ... of families we know very well. The last funeral is in October, which is the eighth one in the seven months since Michael's death.

I feel exhausted and am sure I cannot face another funeral.

Depression is over me like a black cloud and as I leave the Church after the funeral service, a visiting priest, who knows me, says "Hello, how are you now?" I reply, "I'm no good. No good at all!"

He answers, "Still?"

It was only one word but I am I undone for days! I cannot stop crying and am now convinced – nobody, just nobody understands the grief one feels when you lose a child. Someone who has never suffered it says, "Maybe you haven't accepted God's will yet?"

"What is acceptance?" I wondered. "Not crying? Not missing my son?" I became very confused and questioned my Faith.

I explained these feelings to another Priest, and what he says to me in return, allays my fears that something is wrong with me.

He says, "It is only human nature to miss and grieve for Michael. Even though you have accepted God's will, you still miss Michael's presence. This is only a natural feeling and there is nothing wrong with that."

I feel a sense of relief after talking to the Priest and it makes me realise we have to talk out our tormented thoughts to let healing even start to take place.

Here is another view of the positive impact of talking out your conflicting feelings, and how meaningful it can be when your faith helps to clarify even your most painful feelings like shame and despair – faith and feelings stand together hand in hand.[18]

WHAT SHALL I DO WITH THE SHAME?

What shall I do with my shame, Lord?
It's pressing me down into death;
it's squeezing the life from my soul
and stifling the Spirit's sweet breath.
I can't face my friends anymore, Lord
it's harder to face even You.
Though I know all my sins are forgiven,
it's a message that's not getting through.

I'm stuck in a pit – at the bottom
and everything's piling on top.
I know that I should keep on walking
but it's easier to sit and just stop.
You're my Saviour and friend at all times, Lord.
I love You and honour Your name.
I have walked in Your ways many years, Lord,
but what shall I do with this shame?

Then, through my anguish, a voice gently said,

"Remember the Lamb who was cruelly led,
yet willingly lay down His life for your sin?
Well, the guilt and the shame were then placed upon Him.
'It is finished!' He cried as He carried your shame.
He will carry it still if you'll call on His name.
So – climb out of your pit and lift high His name.
The Lord, in His mercy, has dealt with your shame."

CHAPTER 8

AT A GLANCE

- When death intimidates us, religious people and even those who would not describe themselves as followers of a formal faith, may turn to "religious" messages when searching for answers or words intended to comfort.

- Some religious clichés carry an underlying message which implies that death was part of God's design and so we should "grin and bear it". Any message, religious or otherwise, which restricts the flow of natural feelings is unhelpful.

- Faith is not a substitute for feelings, especially those of hurt, anger and disappointment.

- If our friend expresses anger towards God we don't need to come to his rescue. God does not need us to defend him. God understands our human feelings and behaviours.

CHAPTER 9

WHEN DO YOU CALL IN PROFESSIONAL HELP?

If you really are worried about the person you know who is grieving or feel that a greater level of help is needed, ask if he or she would consider talking to a counsellor – you could offer to make the appointment or drive them there and be on hand if they don't want to be alone.

Don't be surprised if you find some opposition to having counselling. Some people believe that you must be crazy if you need professional help. This is a nonsensical notion if we consider it in terms of other forms of help we seek – if we have a problem with a sore tooth, poor eyesight or a nagging pain we consult the appropriate professional.

Psychiatrists, psychologists and counsellors are basically trained as problem solvers – not in the sense that they can make them disappear, but they should have the skills to help their client examine the problem, see if there are other ways of looking at it and then establish the means to manage it more easily or live with it more comfortably.

Effective counsellors develop a relationship with their client firstly by listening to their story and using empathy to develop rapport and establish trust. Then, together, counsellor and client can work towards developing some choices of action that tackle the issues causing concern.

Counselling is particularly helpful when people appear 'stuck' in their grief. One sign of being stuck is a preoccupation with certain feelings like guilt, bitterness or anger which dominate their thinking and consequently their behaviour.

A counsellor can help to examine thinking styles. Sometimes people's thoughts and beliefs about a problem contribute to the size of the problem, making it appear more threatening to them than it really is.

Here is an example:

Luke: *I'm really disappointed in my friends. At the start they said they'd be there for me but now no one comes near me. It's like they've all forgotten. They just don't care.*

Counsellor: *I sense you're feeling let down by a whole lot of people you thought you could depend on.*

Luke: *Yeah. They've dropped me like a hot scone.*

Counsellor: *How would you like your friends to be? What do you expect from them?*

Luke: *Look, I know they're busy and all that but just a call every few weeks. Maybe a beer on the weekend. But they're avoiding me like the plague. And if I'm a bit down and out well maybe they could just let me spill it all out. I don't expect miracles from them – I know they can't bring her back. But just a bit of consideration until I'm on top of things again.*

Counsellor: *Have you told your friends this?*

Luke: *Told them? Outright? I suppose not. I don't want them to get offended. Then no one would come near me.*

Counsellor: *Do you really think "no one would come near you"?*

Luke: *Well, I guess not.*

Counsellor: *Supposing you did tell them, how would your life be different?*

Luke: *I reckon it would sort out the sheep from the goats. I'd find out pretty quick who my real friends were.*

Counsellor: *Amongst your friends, is there someone who you could choose to mention this to first, you know, to test the water?*

In this way the counsellor has helped clarify the problem, examine some solutions and begin Luke on the task of setting some tasks for himself to tackle those uneasy friends. Luke thought that he couldn't alter his predicament but now he knows that he could try to mention the way he feels to just one person first and see what reaction he gets, then try some more, rather than believe it was completely out of the question to speak up.

Crooked thinking is another way some people colour their thoughts and consequent view of the world – *I'll never be happy again. My life has been ruined forever. I'll never survive this.* When people are grieving it's easy for them to think they will never get over it. Thoughts go through their head that say things will never be the same. And they're right. Life will never be exactly the same as before, but that doesn't mean it has to be miserable forever just because it's intolerable right now. It's hard to believe this, but it's true.

One of the lessons grieving people will need to learn is that your life as you knew it has changed. What was your 'normal' life is now gone. But a 'new normal' will emerge. Grieving people would do well to remember this but of course they can't when their head is filled with questions, shock, fear and all the rest of their grief. Their focus is on what is lost, what will never be. This can lead to "catastrophising" – a complete preoccupation with negativity and doom. It can be expressed like this:

His face is going to haunt me for the rest of my life.

I'm never going to smile again.

I will never, ever come to terms with this.

I will never get close to anyone again.

My life is over. I have nothing left to live for.

Such expressive despair does not normally alarm me and I accept it as a fairly accurate perception in early grief. As time passes, the bereaved realise they can join in with life again, even though it can be threatening at first and they are on unfamiliar ground.

Again, a counsellor can use specific challenging skills to clarify the difference between catastrophic beliefs and the real facts. The truth is that most people do learn to smile again and bring happiness back into their lives. But a severe dose of negative thinking on top of a pile of grief will make it harder to believe that this is possible.

Counsellors and similar therapists can also teach *mindfulness* – a helpful way of training ourselves to be aware of unhelpful thoughts which affect our wellbeing. As we become aware of our thoughts, it becomes clear that often the stories we tell ourselves contribute to our unhappiness. Mindfulness has its roots in Eastern philosophy, particularly Buddhist meditation. The aim is to help you be aware of your thoughts and bodily sensations when you are stressed or troubled, and in doing so, help you cope better on a day to day basis.

When you practice mindfulness, you deliberately draw attention away from a worrying or fearful thought, and as you breathe in and out slowly, you observe and accept the present situation, without judging it to be good or bad – it just is. You purely acknowledge your feelings and accept they are real and natural, rather than try to fight them or be critical of yourself for having them. You try to stay focussed on what you can control, not the things you can't.

Mindfulness requires practice because, for many of us, it means learning to change old habits of the way we think. But small steps is how change occurs. Practising mindfulness to deal with sadness or anxiety might simply sound like this, repeated several times, even while you are going for a walk:

Breathing in, I accept my feelings. Breathing out, I calm my feelings.

Sometimes, all that a counsellor needs to do is to reassure the grieving person that their grief is not weird and that they are not going crazy. Because grief can cause so many new and sometimes frightening reactions, some grieving people are quick to conclude that there is something drastically wrong with them. When friends encourage this idea by saying or implying that all this grief is going on for too long, it's easy to be convinced that they're 'losing their marbles'. In such cases, the counsellor can not only clarify what real grief is about but offer strategies to handle those well-meaning friends. On more than one occasion I have seen the enormous relief of someone sitting opposite me when told that their grief sounded normal – the problem lay in their perception of how they should be, rather than in the grief itself. Sometimes, just knowing this means they can stop worrying about whether they are normal and instead accept that this is how their grief is.

An effective counsellor can therefore play a vital role in the helping network of supportive family, friends, employer and so on. But what can counsellors do that others may not be able to do? Basically, they can apply problem solving skills systematically and exhaustively from a viewpoint that is objective and not aimed at 'curing the grief' but rather by examining all the aspects that are affecting it. I don't believe that grieving people ask or even want this from a friend. Friends are possibly expected to do no more than simply 'be there'. But if grief becomes unresolved, exaggerated, prolonged, delayed or complicated in any way, it's time to look for further help.

Here is an explanation to help us identify some of the characteristics of complicated grief. [19]

Complicated grievers remember the past and imagine the future through a distressed yearning for the deceased, hopelessness about the future, waves of painful emotion, and preoccupation with memories of the deceased. This intense preoccupation makes it difficult for them to recall past and future events that do not include the deceased loved one. It is like all other memories that do not include the deceased are erased from their minds ... reflections on the future solely centre on what life would be like if the deceased loved one was still with them.

It's normal to yearn the loss of a loved one ... But these yearning reactions dissipate as mourners work through their feelings about the loss and integrate the loss into their lives.

But complicated grievers keep the yearning process alive through their habits. They may create shrines of the deceased, constantly look at their pictures, or talk about them constantly. What's significant here, is that complicated grievers do not permit space in their lives for anything else but their memories of the lost loved one.

It's important to note that sometimes we can be too quick to describe grief as complicated. I've even seen counsellors do this. Allowing enough time for readjustment is vital, especially when the death is particularly significant. I recall a man who rang me after being told by a psychiatrist that he would feel better about his toddler's death if he stopped carrying around a framed photo of him. The man was perplexed. The photo was all he had left. As the boy had only died a few months prior, I could see no harm in what this father was doing. It was too early for a diagnosis of unresolved, prolonged or complicated grief. But if we believe grief should be over in a few months or that keeping personal possessions just act as morbid reminders, then inappropriate advice could be offered.

Similarly, on another occasion, I received a phone call from a health care worker who was seeking some help for a grieving mother "who just wasn't getting over it". I was told of her preoccupation, above all, with going to the cemetery to visit the grave of her stillborn child. When I asked how long this had been going on, the reply was "since Christmas". It was now March! Again, the real problem lay with the helpers and their idea of what was normal. To allow a mere three months for this mother to be on top of things was not only unfair but insensitive as well. I had a hunch that this mother chose to go to the cemetery not only to be 'near' her child, but also to get away from hurtful comments from people who had no inkling of her real needs. I doubt she was helped by being labelled as 'not coping', nor would she be likely to share her real feelings with anyone who she sensed had no idea of what she was going through.

When it comes to understanding the bottom line of grief, a professional's credentials may not be enough. The making of a good counsellor, like a good helper, begins with genuineness and respect towards the client. Even with the essential skills of non-judgemental listening, empathetic responding, and a common sense and creative approach to problem solving, a counsellor with only a text-book knowledge of grief will be limited in his understanding of the 'nitty gritties' that are unique to each separate loss. It's important to check out more than the training and qualifications of a professional helper – their actual experience in grief counselling is important too.

In recent years, self-help or support groups have evolved out of a need for people to share similar, and usually difficult, life experiences. If we look at a grief support group, one of the greatest benefits for members is that there is no need to explain or justify your feelings to others – they are readily understood. People who attend meetings for help are often relieved to find so many others who share similar thoughts and feelings. A sense of kinship can develop very easily amongst people who learn they are 'not alone' or 'not going mad'. Seeing similarly bereaved people who have survived a year or two, or twenty years down the track can generate much courage and hope for someone whose grief is still new.

I can still remember my first night at the support group. I arrived on my own and hesitated in the doorway. The leader came over, put his hand on my shoulder and invited me inside. Few people amongst my friends were willing to get that close to me – as if they would catch 'death' from me. Meeting after meeting I heard how others coped with situations that I was facing too. Maybe I wasn't so weird after all. How different our stories all were and yet how similar our anxieties and feelings turned out. Often after the meetings I'd be a bit raw again for the next few days but it was worth it for those few hours each month when I felt so completely understood.

Michael had been gone two and a half years, when I read an article in the paper about "The Compassionate Friends" – an international, non-denominational, non-profit organisation for bereaved parents ... this was the first time I'd heard of such an organisation ... I'd felt an urge to speak with one of the mothers who was starting the chapter ... When I first spoke, I told the lady that I too had lost a son. I remember she asked, "How long is it since your son died?"

I replied, "Two and a half years".

Then I was lifted right up when I heard her say, "That isn't very far down the road of grief, is it?"

She didn't say, "You should be feeling a whole lot better by now". I began to cry – something I had been able to keep in control for a while now, but I knew it was all understood ... [20]

Like professional help, support groups can vary in their effectiveness. To be able to offer the best care to its members, a support group should be run by leaders who are trained in grief awareness, empathy, basic counselling skills and small group management. It is essential to have the right 'people skills' to be able to handle different personalities and conduct discussions so that they are positive and aimed towards self-understanding. If a leader allows a group meeting to become nothing but a time to complain about all those thoughtless people out there, then week in week out group members will do no more than go around in circles.

The intention of a support group should not be to create a group of 'bereaved parents' or 'grieving widows' who see themselves as separate from the non-bereaved population. Sure, their experience of loss has given them issues to deal with that some people know nothing about. But the idea of working through their grief should be to find ways of becoming a part of the world they used to live in rather than getting involved in activities which make them even more isolated.

If your friend is considering attending a self-help group, it would be wise to check out its objectives and find out how facilitators are selected and trained. It is also advisable to enquire how they liaise with the network of professional counsellors and other resource people in your local community.

Sometimes it will be talk of suicide that will prompt the help of a professional. It is not unusual for a grieving person to speak in terms of wanting to be dead. This may be expressed in words like:

I can't live without him.

I've got nothing left to live for.

My life will never be the same. I just want to die too.

Over the years, I have heard variations along this same theme from almost every bereaved person I have spoken with. They describe their grief in terms of "just wanting to hear their voice once more" or "just to be able to hold him or her again". Although it is often expressed as a death wish, I listen to the message behind the words and the message usually just says that they want to be with that person in the way it used to be. The message doesn't mean they want to be dead – they actually want to be *alive* together enjoying all the things they used to.

The dilemma for the helper comes from not knowing when the words *I'd rather be dead* really do mean *I'm going to kill myself* or if they mean *I'm sick of all this grief, I want it all to go away.*

You need to arm yourself with information about suicide so that you are in a better position to help your friend. Suicide warning signs may be a cry for help and give family and friends the opportunity to seek professional help and intervention.

Sometimes people give no signs of contemplating suicide, but you must take comments like these seriously:

You won't have to put up with me soon.

You'll be better off without me.

When I'm gone I won't bother you anymore.

There is no evidence to suggest that by asking a suicidal person if they are thinking about ending their life that you will actually put the idea into their head.[21] In reality, it shows how carefully you have listened and how perceptive you are about their situation. By being able to talk with you frankly about all this, your friend also knows that they can come to you no matter how bad they are feeling. You have let them know they don't have to carry their grief alone, and that's a good feeling when you think no one has any time for you or your problems.

Be aware of suicide warning signs: [22]

They may give away their possessions and get their affairs in order.

They may say their goodbyes.

They may begin to withdraw from contact with their circle of friends.

They may engage in dangerous or risky behaviour.

They may increase their use of alcohol or drugs.

They may talk or write about death or suicide (and it's out of character for them).

They may hint at how they will end their life or tell you of their suicide plan:

I know where Dad keeps his gun.
or
I've got enough tablets to make sure it works.

They may show several signs of depression:

Loss of interest in usual activities.

Showing signs of sadness, hopelessness, anxiety, agitation.

Change in appetite or weight.

Changes in sleep patterns; sleeping longer, shorter or broken sleep.

Loss of energy; tiredness or irritability.

Making negative comments about themselves; low self esteem.

Finding it hard to concentrate; restlessness.

Having suicidal thoughts or death fantasies that are recurrent.

It is noteworthy that even depressed people rarely take their own lives because of a singular crisis. Usually, an overload of difficult events or a tipping point is the trigger, coupled with a feeling of being defeated by their circumstances. If you want to know if your friend is seriously considering suicide, you'll only find out if you ask. This means you will have to come right out with questions like:

Have you felt like you've wanted to join him?

Are you so lonely that you would think of killing yourself?

Are you thinking of suicide? Have you been planning how you would do it?

Do not ask like this: *You're not going to do something stupid, are you?*

Remember, asking sensitively does not put the idea of suicide into someone's mind. Sure you can't be a minder and watch your friend's every move, but you may be able to spend more time together – maybe some company will help fill in those lonely hours. Watch a movie together, listen to music, walk and talk together, or buy your friend a journal and suggest they could write about their feelings – it doesn't matter if they're all muddled up – as long as they come out. Or you could give your friend the telephone number of a 24 hour counselling service like Lifeline – just in case you can't be reached at a time when he or she really needs someone.

When grieving people reach a really low point, 'staying with their feelings' is one of the most important things you can do. Unfortunately, I have often seen family and friends become so exasperated at this

point that they do the opposite. Some try to bully the grieving person
out of their feelings:

It's time you stopped living in the past and pulled yourself together.

You're just feeling sorry for yourself.

What a lot of rubbish! You've got years of life in you yet.

Or they try to make them feel guilty and selfish:

Think about the rest of us instead of just yourself.

You're not the only one that's hurting, you know.

There are others who have been through worse than you.

What can actually happen now for the grieving person is that their
perception of being alone, misunderstood and surrounded by people
who don't care, is verified. So the 'helpful' intentions backfire, possibly
leaving more grief in their wake. Don't be afraid to tell your friend that
you are worried about them and that you want to find someone more
experienced to help. You could put it like this:

*It really worries me when you are so down. I'd like to find someone to
help you.*

*I'm scared because I don't know how to help you. I'd like to talk to someone
who knows about these things.*

I'm going to stick by you and want to find a way together to work this out.

Then follow up by checking out resources in your area and making
telephone enquiries yourself. If you come across someone you think
could help further you could suggest to your friend that you would be
willing to go with them, or just wait in the car during the appointment.

Maybe both of you could even be helped if you were able to discuss the situation together and learn some ways to deal with them. On the internet, there are excellent, easy to read tip sheets on all aspects of suicide – you could print these and talk about them with your friend. Do stay in touch, try to spend some time with them – people rarely suicide in company. Even sending a daily text message to check in with your friend says that someone is thinking about them, someone cares.

Here is a practical example to consider based on a real family's experience. I received a telephone call which went something like this:

"Our son was killed a couple of months ago and my wife just isn't handling it at all and she keeps saying that she'd rather be dead. We're really worried about her. Can you come over and talk to her?"

I was shown into the kitchen when I arrived. Grief hung in the air. I didn't ask *How are you?* My eyes could see how they were. The family was introduced to me – Mum, Dad and two daughters. Their only son and brother was killed in an industrial accident – a job he had only had for a week.

To understand the whole picture of this family's loss, I directed my first question at them all, *"Can you tell me what happened on the day he died?"* They recounted his last hours on the job. He was examining some equipment. There was an explosion. He was seriously injured. A mercy dash to hospital. A phone call – your son's been hurt. Come at once. The bedside vigil. The injuries were too severe and he died while the rest of the world celebrated Valentine's Day.

For an hour or so they continued. I sensed a very strong bond between mother and son. He was the eldest child. He was the subsequent baby after a stillborn son. He was the most successful of the three children at school and in his job. He was a good sportsman. He was everybody's friend. He kept his room tidy. He didn't swear or smoke or drink to excess. He was a caring big brother to his sisters. He was great company when Dad was too busy with work. In effect, he fitted the bill of a perfect son.

With this perfection torn out of her life, his mother believed she was stripped of her reason for living. She knew she could never find perfection like this in anyone again. Her husband could not fill his shoes, her daughters could not, nobody could. She had surrounded herself with his photographs – they could be seen from every angle in the room. This was all she had left. She longed to be with her boy. She longed to see his smile and longed to hear his voice. If she were dead too her longing would be over.

What can you say when you hear a story like this? It just didn't seem right for me to say:

At least you've still got your two lovely girls.

or

Who's going to look after this beautiful home and family if you're not around?

or

They say God only takes the best – and he sure was the best son you could have asked for.

Your first task as a helper is to show you have listened. So frame a response which acknowledges how much this son mattered. It could sound something like this:

"Your son really meant the world to you. He was such a big part of your life. I can see how proud you were of him and that you miss him so much it seems unbearable. Even with everyone here who loves you, there's a huge gap that the others just can't fill."

Then, the family could also be helped with an explanation of grief and the way it affects individuals differently, even though they are mourning the loss of the same person. The grief that Mum was feeling was so intense that wanting to escape the hurt was natural.

After all, who wants to wake up every day knowing that nothing but emptiness was waiting for you? The idea of being dead meant that at least you weren't being hounded by your feelings and the memories which jumped out of every nook and cranny in the house. Such an explanation isn't saying *Go ahead and kill yourself*, it's simply letting them know that Mum was carrying a huge load of grief which was weighing her down and tearing at her will to live.

I suspect if I had asked each person in the room to draw up an inventory of what they missed most, what mattered most in their relationship with him and what hurt most, no two lists would be identical. Mum's grief was similar to theirs and yet it was so unlike theirs. That's why she expressed her pain differently and that's why it was difficult for others to comprehend.

As a helper, it's important that you convey that you do understand. You don't know how they feel, but you can understand why their feelings are so intense and you can see why their world has been torn apart. This would not be achieved in this example if Mum were told: *"Stop dwelling on it. Don't be so selfish and think of your family. Your son wouldn't want you to be carrying on like this"*. In reality, she had heard all these clichés and they weren't making her feel any better. If anything, she was angry with the people who just couldn't grasp how great her loss was. They hadn't stood in her shoes and found out how close the ties were between mother and son. They had heard her words but not understood the feelings behind them. By 'staying with her feelings' you would be able to establish the essential foundations for building trust and inviting further communication.

So, if the grieving person you know is feeling guilty, let him talk about his guilt. If there's intense hostility, let him express his anger and frustration. If there's talk of unbearable loneliness, let him tell you what he misses most. Giving permission for these feelings won't make them worse – it will actually get the emotions out in the open where they can begin to dissipate. When this happens, grieving people begin to learn that they can hang on, even though they are 'in the pits' at the present time. Your role is to remain calm and provide a safe environment where it is permissible to tell your story the way it really is.

CHAPTER 9

AT A GLANCE

- A professional counsellor has specific skills to help clients with a problem, especially when they have run out of ideas or motivation or feel like they are getting nowhere on their own.

- The need for grief counselling is not a sign of weakness or being 'crazy'. Grief can become complicated and hard to resolve on your own – this is the right time to seek professional help.

- Don't ignore anyone who is talking about ending their life. By telling you this they are begging for help. Talk about it openly. Don't keep it a secret – tell them you want to get some professional help for them.

- Support groups have the potential to offer a degree of understanding for the bereaved that is often lacking in the rest of the community.

CHAPTER 10

HOW LONG WILL ALL THIS GRIEVING LAST?

I have already mentioned that there are misconceptions about the length of time grieving takes. Some people think that the worst of your grief will be over after the funeral but many people are still enveloped in shock at that time and the real impact is yet to be felt. Then there are those who say, "Give it a year and then you'll be over it." Well I've heard many grieving people tell me that the second year was worse than the first!

On the other hand, some people say "Time is a great healer" but I have seen little evidence of this. What I have seen is that as time moves on, most grieving people learn to adapt to the changes in their lives, with some adjusting better and quicker than others. But time didn't do the adjusting, they did it themselves. I have also met first hand some people who never really adjusted to their loss. Sure, on the outside they appear to have coped – they're back at work, they're married again, they have a new family or built a new house or go about their business as usual but their pain is simply buried, not healed. I don't even like that word 'healed'. It implies that the pain has been removed or cut out or stitched up so that it won't cause any more trouble. Like a wound that has healed. But when you're wounded by grief it's very different.

What I see amongst people who have grieved is that they find ways of making their lives meaningful again alongside the knowledge that they will never forget – it's like having an invisible scar which is evidence that a wound was once there. Sometimes remembering might cause them to be sad, and often their memories will make them glad. But they'll always remember. What will make them mad however, is being told to forget. I have never met a grieving person who wanted to forget the person who died. They might want to forget the circumstances of the death like the scene of the accident or a body twisted in pain, but they don't want to forget the actual person.

So there is no need for friends to go about purposely 'helping' them forget by immediately removing all the belongings or putting away photographs or not saying their name. Remember, getting through your grief is not about forgetting, it's about finding ways of living with your memories, living with the truth and living through the ups and downs of each day as time keeps moving on.

Time never heals, you just go on each day because it's expected of you to 'get on with life'.

We had our next son a year later and I would say the cracks were papered over by the impact of him in our lives. The very fact of my tears as I write to you now, 14 years later, suggests my grief is still rolling through the back alleys of my mind.

So much has changed in the world since he left. Like time is forever marked as before and after his death.

I see a big difference between fresh grief and grief that has been influenced by time. When grief is new, it gets in the way of almost everything the bereaved think and do. They wake up and it's there. They go to sleep and it's still there. It's like their grief is controlling their lives. But as they deal with their feelings, grieving people slowly win back that control so that they can choose when they want to walk through the 'back alleys' of their grief and I have a hunch that it's more like a sentimental stroll than a weary trudge, knee deep in snags, ambushed by memories and trapped by feelings.

When the bereaved are expected to pretend that their loss is not so bad, they have no hope of having their grief identified and validated, both of which must happen if it is to be resolved. Here is an example of how one family tried to deal with their grief which had not gone away even though eleven years had passed since their son's death. The following is a letter which they sent to their family and friends:

When Caleb, our first child, died soon after a premature birth, in 1976, we were shocked.

We were so unprepared that the reality of what had happened scarcely sank in.

The birth of our other three boys made us realise just what we had lost and then Bartholomew's death in 1985 made us reflect on how we had dealt with Caleb's death and burial.

We now wish we had held a service and therefore we will be holding a Memorial Service for Caleb in the Children's Section of the Colac Lawn Cemetery at 2pm on Sunday, January 25, the eleventh anniversary of his death.

This family's hidden grief was exposed when another death occurred in their lives. After much indecision, they chose to bring their feelings out into the open – a real risk in our society where we urge people to forget rather than remember. Together with a clergyman, I officiated at the memorial service and they chose these words to explain why it is necessary to finally put things right:

Some may question why this memorial service should be held so many years after the event. But to me the answer is clear. It is the culmination of an eleven year journey for Dot and Rod – a journey which began with shock and disbelief and which was complicated by the attitudes of society which said – "Don't mourn, keep yourself busy, have another baby, you'll get over it." These messages were reinforced even further by professionals who also did not understand the process of grief and more importantly the bond which exists between a mother, a father and their new baby. The relationship between parent and infant is powerful; in any event a lasting attachment has been formed that endures in strength for years and years.

Then with the unexpected stillbirth of their fifth son Bartholomew, the grief work which had barely begun for Caleb was reactivated and finally faced. There were many questions still to be asked, some with no answers, many documents to be searched, procedures to be queried, gaps to be filled

*and most importantly, a life to be recognised. A small human being had
to be acknowledged.*

*I feel it is important to stress that Dot and Ron are not alone in what they
have experienced. In my work as a funeral director I have, on a number of
occasions, been faced with similar parents who were searching for evidence
of a child long dead and never acknowledged. These are parents who knew
they had the right to grieve but were still awaiting permission from those
around them.*

Memory triggers are another issue for the bereaved which can trip
them up just when they thought they had a grip on things. Sometimes
we're prepared for obvious triggers like special days on the calendar –
Christmas, birthdays, anniversaries, family celebrations. But there are
other triggers like favourite colours, songs, smells, TV shows, food …
seeing a car that's the same as your loved one's or hearing someone else
called by their name. Favourite places, your regular café or just seeing
couples or families spending time together – these can trigger memories
when you too shared happy times like these.

*After my baby died, I hated the supermarket aisle where they kept the babies
things. All those tins of food and powder and stuff just reminded me that he
was gone. I hated being reminded right in the middle of shopping.*

*Sometimes when I'm shopping and I see friends walking around with their
Mums I think 'What about me? Why haven't I got a Mum?'*

*Setting the table is one of the hardest things I have to do. It doesn't sound
like much but when you've set five places for all those years and now there
are only four it just gets to you.*

*It was five years since she died but on the day I saw all those little kids line
up for their first day at school and mine wasn't there, I was miserable all
day. It just wasn't fair, she should have been lining up too.*

Maureen McCormack's poem shows how the loss of ordinary day to day conversation is her daily reminder that her husband is 'not there':

You know those little things that happen
The things you always like to share?

I go to tell you of them
But forget that you're not there.

I think I must tell you something I heard
A little bit of gossip or just a little word

Sometimes I have a thing I must share
But forget that you're not there.

Someone I met or saw at the shops
I must tell you I think, but there the thought stops

No, no more can I share
I must try and remember
That you are no longer there.

Then there are those days which come around every year, bringing with them reminders, memories and very often a silent vigil of remembrance:

In those first few years I watched the calendar like a hawk. It was telling me how long we've lived without her. That first anniversary was the pits but the second and third weren't much better. When the actual day came it wasn't as bad as the past days of my private count-down but every hour or so I was calculating – this time last year we were still together. Then an hour later I'd look at the clock and think, this time last year I was putting you down for your nap. Then that time which I dreaded would come – the time last year when you were gone.

On Wayne's accident anniversary I do not go to work. Always I will go to him, talk to him and love him dearly. Also I wear the same dress on the 14th of February as I had on when I saw him last in hospital.

I have often wondered why it is acceptable to publicly remember wartime deaths or those which resulted from natural disasters, terrorism or large scale accidents. Not one year has gone by since Elvis Presley's death or the shooting of John Lennon or President John F. Kennedy or Princess Diana's fatal accident or the collapse of the Twin Towers in New York without the 6 o'clock news showing us a flashback to the events and the continuing grief of loyal followers and fans or those affected. Every year, the media tells us that Anzac Day ceremonies get bigger and bigger with thousands of people publicly remembering.

But to remember your own stillborn baby year after year is somehow treated as an odd thing in our society. Shouldn't you be trying to forget? To talk about a spouse or parent who has died may be met with an awkward silence. Shouldn't you be trying to put that behind you? Birthdays, a wedding anniversary, festive times like Christmas, Easter, Mother's Day and Father's Day, holidays, the anniversary of the death and more are significant days for most grieving people. By allowing a grieving friend to remember on these days we do a special thing for them. We actually join them in saying, "This person really mattered to you."

After all, if we allow people to remember a tragedy that occurred in another part of the world, to people who they don't even know, why is it so bizarre that a friend should want to remember their child, partner, parent, whoever? You know what I think? Outsiders believe that the bereaved are remembering the death, even dwelling on it. Sure, they can't forget that the person has died, but I believe they are also remembering what was significant about knowing that person. They are remembering someone who mattered. Remembering in itself is not a sign of unresolved grief. It is as much a mark of respect as it is an annual observance.

What can a friend do at times like these? Make contact – text, email or phone – let your message say something like 'I remember too'. Or you can endorse the idea to do something special on a significant day rather than raise your eyebrows in disapproval. At the cemetery where our daughter is buried, whenever I visit at Easter I often see chocolate eggs or bunnies placed on some of the graves and at Christmas time, there will be little Santa trinkets or angels or bells. Now, I never choose to do more than place some flowers but that doesn't mean other parents cannot do what they feel they have to do. If there is any guideline that applies at all here, it is, do what you feel is right for you. I know of other families who bake a birthday cake and sing a round of *Happy Birthday* to commemorate a family member who has died. These are simply ways people stay connected to someone who mattered. It's not a cause for concern, these are examples of how people preserve 'continuing bonds'.

This is how two teenage boys stayed 'connected' to their brother when he died:

We notice that Peter spends a lot of time after school lying on Mick's bed and playing with his walking stick, even sleeping in the bed on a number of occasions, with his brother Chris ... Mickey would be so happy that the boys were not frightened of his room.[23]

When I do the washing, nothing seems to have changed. Peter and Chris are wearing Mick's shirts and shorts ... we did not go through Mick's clothes as some do shortly after a person dies, as Mick had bequeathed them to his brothers who were already wearing them.[24]

I always visit Tristan's grave on his birthday and leave red roses. Roses were the flowers Janine and I chose for his coffin. Janine planted a rose to commemorate him and still nurtures it in a pot. I regularly collect a flower and now have dried roses for each year since his birth.

One evening at dinner, my husband suggested we make some plans to include our daughter, Ashleigh, in our traditional Easter celebrations. Our two sons were delighted and it also opened up all new avenues to remember their sister. I can remember the tension lifting as we spoke of our ideas. In the end, our brief conversation provided a kind of peace and

acceptance of our loss. That Easter will always hold a precious place in our hearts. The boys, once again were able to enjoy the coming holiday. They dyed Easter eggs and lovingly decorated two for their sister. We ordered a beautiful posy of pink and white flowers for her grave and placed it there after attending Easter Sunday service. Tyler and Derek carefully placed their eggs next to the bouquet. We all said some special words, shed some tears, hugged, took some photos and believe it or not, we even felt proud of our accomplishments. We went on to celebrate together, speaking freely for the first time in many months.

We always say Grace at the dinner table – I'd have liked our prayer of thanksgiving to have mentioned her name too – anything would have been preferable to that eerie silence that hung over us on that first Christmas.

Sometimes the cemetery is a focal place for family to gather to remember, but some people choose not to be frequent cemetery visitors and this should not be criticised either. Bereaved families do not need a trip to the cemetery to show they have remembered – they are always aware that someone close has died. If you are aware that a significant date is coming up for a friend, the lead up to this time is often worse for the bereaved than the day itself. A visitor who calls in for a chat or brings along a bunch of flowers or a six-pack of beer can be a welcome sight.

Christmas time is often one of the hardest and loneliest times for the bereaved. It's heightened by all the Christmas cheer, festive events and obligation to celebrate because *'tis the season to be jolly'*. It's a time when some people can't bear the thought of writing cards, putting up the tree and doing all the things they used to. If you know someone who will be struggling around Christmas time, give them a call, invite them over for a quiet get-together, suggest they might like to bring a photo of their loved one – have the courage to mention their name, speak up, acknowledge their loss and let them know that you understand that there are memory triggers everywhere of a missing face, an empty chair, and silent thoughts of the way Christmas used to be.

CHAPTER 10

AT A GLANCE

- Getting through grief is not about forgetting – it's about finding ways of living with all the things you remember. It's unfair to say, or imply in any way, that it's alright to remember for a year or maybe two but after that it's time to put it behind you.

- There are times of the year that will bring obvious reminders to your friend that someone special is not there. Don't be afraid to show that you have remembered too.

- Be supportive of a friend's choice to do something particular to acknowledge a birthday or anniversary. It's not self-indulgent or morbid to remember.

- Sometimes, memory triggers can come out of nowhere and make the bereaved feel like they are back to square one. Let them talk about this too.

- It takes considerable time for the bereaved to adapt to life without the person who has died. Staying connected through 'continuing bonds' can help grieving people to adjust and to honour their memory.

CHAPTER 11

WHAT ABOUT CHILDREN?

These days, children are seen more readily at funerals. Yet, many adults still believe that children will be harmed if they are exposed to all the talk and rituals which surround a death in the family – meeting with the funeral director, seeing the person who has died in the coffin, attending the funeral and being present at the cemetery or crematorium.

When we exclude children, we could be doing more harm than good. Why? Because we rob them of opportunities to learn about a natural part of living – that all life eventually comes to an end. We also leave them with many unanswered questions:

Where is my Daddy now?

Why is Mummy sad?

What happened to Grandma?

Older children may be more curious about nuts and bolts issues like:

What does a dead body look like?

How deep is the grave?

Is there really such a place as Heaven?

Children as young as two or three years of age can sense the impact of a death in the family, often signalled by changes in household routines and the appearance of unfamiliar faces. Naturally they are too young to know the real meaning of death, but they are not too young to feel frightened and insecure about the unusual comings and goings in their home.

Around the age of four or five, it will be more difficult to convince children that all is well because they will overhear conversations and their eyes will tell them that people look strained, upset or are not behaving in their usual way. What adults often forget is that children in this age group have seen dead birds in the garden, they have watched TV shows where space heroes kill evil forces, they have listened to stories about fairy tale characters who die (although they may be saved by a handsome prince). They have heard, and probably used, expressions like "drop dead", "dead tired" and when they're in trouble they know they are "dead scared".

An even more realistic death experience for young children is the death of a pet and many will know what a dead cat, dog or kindergarten pet looks like. Yet, when a person dies, adults feel it is necessary to suddenly alter the truth of the event by saying something like:

Grandma has gone to be with the angels.

We lost Pa today.

Daddy has gone to sleep forever.

Your baby brother is a star in the sky.

By distorting the facts, we can unwittingly add an unnecessary dimension to death – mystery – and that confuses and even angers children:

Why did the angels take my Grandma away? I want them to bring her back!

Where is my Pa? Why can't they find him?

When will Daddy wake up? I don't want to go to sleep anymore.

The following selected verses of a poem were written by Shirley Rutherford as an adult, retelling her view of the events at the time of her young brother's death, when she was just two years old.[25]

When I was two you went away
and left me.
I waited every day for you to come,
But you didn't and every day was empty ...

At night in bed I talked to you
begged God to get you back to me
God loves me I know, and knew it then,
but He didn't find you for me.
So I cried inside, no tears, no sound,
Until my throat ached and I couldn't bear
to breathe in case my chest burst.
And I hated God for letting you leave me;
and loved the picture of Sunday School
of Jesus and the children
And hated you for leaving me –
and tried to love you back to me
but still you didn't come.

And then one day I knew that you were gone.
They said the word that told me you had left me –
and all my waiting would have to end.
Dead.
And it rang like a gong that wouldn't stop
vibrating
On and on –
Dead and dead and dead ...

... I felt like an old woman in a body
only eight
Six years of vigil, all alone inside had
made me aged forever,
and that I had to hide.
For children are "so lucky", they're "protected"
from pain of life and love.
"Not understanding" makes it easy
to bounce back, untouched by grief.

When I was two you went away
and left me

And my grief was real and sane.
I could have coped with "dead"
at two or three or four,
But "heaven" is a soft and gentle name
for dead.
At eight my grieving was renewed –
this time for Morris, died aged six.
I'd waited for you longer than you'd lived –
and felt so foolish for not knowing
dead and heaven are the same.

A dangerous effect of telling half-truths to children is that they are left with an incomplete explanation. They will probably rely on their imagination to fill in the missing details – and often fantasy is more fearful or exaggerated than the truth. When adults collaborate to make death and funerals a mysterious event, children may become frightened and uneasy, which can add an extra burden to the sadness or confusion they're experiencing.

I am a witness to this happening in my own family. When my baby daughter Claire died, we did not do a very good job of telling her three year old sister Kate what had happened. We thought she was too young to fully understand and so we initially said her sister became very sick in the night and had to go to hospital. How was I to know that from then on, every time we drove past a hospital, she would ask if the doctor had made her sister better yet? I didn't have an answer for that but somehow changed the story to say that her sister wasn't really in the hospital anymore. Now another problem was emerging – how often would I have to change the story to accommodate the changing questions?

After some time, she invented a ghost which lived in our bedroom wardrobe – it was one of those huge walk-in robes and was always dark and filled with boxes and odds and ends. At night, and only at night, she refused to go down to that part of the house because "the ghost comes out of there when it's dark". I am convinced the "ghost" was her explanation for the reason why her sister disappeared so mysteriously one night – she was literally there at bedtime and by the morning she had vanished. As parents, we never really shed any light on the matter

– we hadn't used the word 'dead' in explaining what had happened to her sister, and we excluded her from the funeral so I guess she came up with her own scenario to explain what makes your baby sister suddenly disappear in the night.

Now, if ever I needed a friend to guide me, this was the time. But not a friend who, like me, thought fairy tales were the answer, but a friend who knew something about children's grief and the way adults should explain death to their own kids. Because there was no one around to help me, I ended up with a sizeable load of guilt about the whole way we handled the matter and in my own mind developed a private "If only ..." list that hounded me for a long time. My list looked something like this:

If only someone had said: *I know you're trying to make it easier for her, but you can't keep pretending that nothing has happened. After all the lead up to the new baby, she will be very aware that she's missing and will sense that something very wrong has happened at your place.*

If only someone had said: *What if we sit her down and tell her together, in simple words that her sister has died. We can explain that something happened which was very, very serious which stopped her breathing and that it only happens to little babies – that way she won't worry about her own breathing or even yours.*

If only someone had said: *Then when you take her to see her sister before the funeral she will see how peaceful she looks and that there's nothing to be scared of. She can see with her own eyes that her sister is lying still, can't move and will not wake up. That will help her to know that dead is different from sleeping.*

If only someone had said: *I can sit with her at the funeral if you like. That way, if she gets restless or asks a question, you won't have to be worried about her. You've got enough to worry about right now.*

If only someone had said: *After the funeral she will see how the coffin is buried so she will begin to learn that this is what happens when a person dies.*

If only someone had said: *I know there are some good books around for kids her age. I'll see if I can get some and you can read them to her to help her understand better. She's bound to have lots more questions over the next few months and they're going to continue as she grows older.*

If only someone had said: *I can see how you're trying to be strong in front of her but it won't harm her to see her parents crying. That way she'll know that she can cry too.*

If only someone had said: *Maybe after a while you could make a scrap book with her about her sister. That way you can talk about her together and look at her photos so that she'll know it's all right to remember.*

I know I have repeatedly said that a friend's role is not to be an advice-giver, but I see a real difference here. When the motive of an advice giver is to make you do things their way, then it is an inappropriate intervention. But when it's based on genuine empathy and sound knowledge and will lead to a better decision or rule out some regrets, then I think a friend should take the risk and speak up.

Before you express your opinions about any matters to do with death and funerals, make sure that what you say is based on what we know to be truly helpful and not simply a repetition of the myths and fears that are still widespread. What you will have to decide for yourself is where to draw the line between butting in with unwanted suggestions and intervening where you can see an outcome which may complicate things later.

How to talk to children about death is just another job which parents aren't trained to do. That means that we may not know what children's grief is about either. Watching the behaviour of children will often give tell-tale clues about their feelings. Aggressive play or actions towards others may signal anger and frustration; not wanting to be left alone or clinging to a parent may mean the child is afraid or feeling insecure; so is reverting to bed wetting, baby talk or not wanting to sleep alone. Being difficult, uncooperative and any attention seeking behaviour may be a child's way of saying that they are feeling left out, confused or scared.

Often the only answer for grieving children is hugs and cuddles – the easiest way of showing they are still loved and will be looked after even in the midst of all this confusion at home. Keeping routines like mealtimes and a story before going to bed can give children the surety they need. Coupled with simple and honest explanations about what has happened, children are less likely to become overloaded with anxiety or fanciful ideas about death.

Don't forget teenagers – it's hard for them to know how to act when someone close has died. Their grief is no less intense or hard to bear than that of an adult and yet it is often dismissed because we assume kids bounce back easily. Listen to these teenagers explaining how the death of someone close affected their lives: [26]

Anger and frustration hit me and I broke nearly everything in my bedroom.

I remember crying so hard that my insides felt like coming out.

I'm still scared of being alone and often sleep with my Mum and Dad.

I felt angry at God for taking her away.

I don't like to be felt sorry for, but just some signs of comfort, some hugs ...

Children and teenagers often draw or write about their day to day experiences and how they feel about them. When they experience a loss, this can be a useful way of examining their response to the event. Kate, aged 11, wrote the following for her English teacher:

BUTTER

Hurt is like a hot knife in butter – it hits you straight in the heart.

Hurt is when playing a joke and hiding from your friends, and then they're really upset and won't talk to you; and the loss of friendship is hard to fill in – like a pit that has no end.

To stop hurt can hurt more. When the person won't listen to you, you are disappointed, you think you will never speak to them again. You think you have no hope to fix up the hurt inside.

Like a hen waiting for her first egg to hatch and the chicken inside is dead. It stings her inside; it may be incurable to think what the chick would have been like; what sort of personality it would have had and she can't think of it until the next chick hatches and then the hurt goes away.

Like the last leaf falling off trees in late autumn and then in spring everything is back again.

But still the fear is there, when the next egg is about to hatch. The hen's anxiety to see the chick that's inside the egg and then she is disappointed – nothing can replace the lost chick – nothing on earth.

What Kate doesn't tell us is that her father died four months earlier, but her story is filled with images of grief which cannot be ignored. Like many children her age, she might not know how to talk openly about her feelings. What if people criticise or laugh at her or say that she should be over it? Writing is often a familiar and safe method for talking things over and, for teenagers, it's important that we hear what their hurt is all about – yes, it does sting and hit you straight in the heart when you're told your father is never coming home again.

Kids like Kate often keep their grief to themselves or are robbed of its recognition by unknowing people around them. Sometimes, when their feelings are so disregarded, like small children, adolescents may also use their behaviour to tell others that they are not happy with the way their world looks. Their grief may become the trigger for so called 'unexplained' anti-social conduct like bullying, swearing, vandalism, disobedience, drug taking and thrill-seeking, risky behaviour.

Here are 12 tips for adults to help children and teens:

1. They need to know they will be cared for in the midst of a crisis – help them feel safe

2. They need to know they did not cause the death/divorce by their thoughts or behaviour

3. They need clear information with age appropriate language

4. They need to ask questions – keep the door open, invite and expect ongoing questions

5. They need to grieve – talk about feelings, fears, fantasies

6. They need to see adults model 'good grief' behaviour

7. They need to be invited to attend and, if they wish, participate in farewells

8. They need to be allowed to remember – make a scrapbook, keep a journal, create a video or photo story

9. They need to have keepsakes – would they like something to keep that is special to them?

10. They may need to revisit what the loss means to them – it will change as they get older

11. They need your understanding – more empathy, less advice

12. They need you to know that sometimes their grief is disguised by "bad" behaviour – punishment or ridicule is not the answer. They need your attention, try talking and finding out what's at the bottom of it all.

Here are some children telling us just what they need in their own words: [27]

I want to know – What did he die of? Where did he die? How long ago did he die? How was he cremated? Why was I not allowed to see him dead? What did he look like when he was dead? Did he go blue?
– Katrina, aged 10.

When I was sent out so the adults could talk, I was curious about what they were talking about. Were they talking about something that might happen?
– Steve, aged 11

You should tell parents to ask children why they are sad. And if they are sad themselves they should tell their child that they are sad too. Then the child will know that she is not the only one. – Nancy, aged 9

For adults to understand the way a child is thinking they should talk normally as if the child was a person – and not too young to understand.
– Christine, aged 10

If your grieving friend has children it's important for you to know all this. Parents can become so overloaded with their own feelings, that they have little patience or energy to deal with everybody else's grief. In addition, they probably won't know what to expect from their children – one child may cry openly while another appears unaffected and keeps on playing or watching television.

You can help further by:

• Doing some housework, shopping, cooking or gardening which will give your friend more time to spend with the children.

- Allowing your friend some time-out by taking the children for a walk, to the movies or to your house for an overnight stay. But, be cautious about forcing children to be separated from their mother or father – all they may want right now is to be with Mum or Dad, regardless of how topsy-turvy the household has become.

- Remembering that the children may be feeling left out or overlooked. A hug, some special words from you, or bringing around their favourite dessert are all ways of saying: *You haven't been forgotten.*

- Letting the child know that their grief matters too. Perhaps you could buy a photo frame and suggest that it's for a favourite picture of the person (or pet) who died. Or buy a journal and say it could help to write about the person who died and how you feel about it.

It is also worth noting that bereaved parents will probably gain little comfort from being told that their other children, especially young ones, will soon forget the child who died and won't therefore be overly affected by this upheaval in the family. Just as parents themselves don't want to forget, neither will they want this for their other children. For parents, this only serves to diminish the value and meaning of their child's place in the family:

Comments that hurt came from the ones that said Amy is young and she will forget and not remember this bad loss of her sister Jess. This I think was the worst comment of all. After 12 months, Amy still talks of Jess nearly every day as we both do. She has lots of good and bad and sad things she talks about and people never give kids the credit of their memory at this age.

And just recently we sold Jessie's cot and on the day the lady came to pick it up Amy became really upset. She cried and didn't want to see it go. We tried to explain why we didn't need it any more but we could see she was angry with us for selling it. It took her ages to calm down and by bed time we thought it was all forgotten. Next morning, as soon as she woke up, her first words to us were, "You're not going to sell Jessie's bike too, are you?" Amy is just 4 years old but don't tell us that little kids don't have any feelings.

CHAPTER 11

AT A GLANCE

- It can be a natural response of adults to try to protect children from information and involvement when a family member has died. Sometimes though, children perceive this as being 'left out' and use their imaginations to fill in the missing pieces of a story.

- When explaining that a pet or a person has died, try to stick to real words rather than 'nice' but misleading information.

- Children have feelings too – what may be missing is their ability to tell us about them. Look for changed or inappropriate behaviour – sometimes this is a child's way of saying that they are scared or need our attention.

- Children learn from observing others around them. When they see adults swallowing their tears, or hear words that say you should be brave in front of other people then they may learn that this is the correct way to be when you are sad.

- By attending a funeral, a child learns what really happens to a body after death. While it can be sad to be there, it can also be a way of finding out that what you see on TV, the internet or science fiction books is not necessarily what happens in real life.

- You can show children that you are aware that they are hurting too by doing something special, yet unobtrusive, just for them.

CHAPTER 12

EMPATHY IS ALSO ABOUT YOUR ACTIONS

While I've given much attention to what you can say, don't forget the worthwhile things you can do. Just by turning up, your presence tells your friend, you are not alone in this. You are being remembered. Here is one mother's recollection:

The love of our friends and even people we did not know sustained us and gave us strength, when at times we were at our lowest ebb through Michael's illness. For instance …

… the friend, who drove all over town to buy water ice-blocks, and at another time, pineapple and strawberries – because that's what Michael had fancied

… Dear Beat, who would drop in a batch of hot scones just out of the oven on her way to town

… the young lad who, when learning Michael needed lemons to have in his new treatment, rode out on his motorbike into the country to pick some

… the neighbour who sat with Mick enabling me to go to the hairdressers

… dear Bev who arrived with fillets of steak and bacon and eggs, especially for Michael

… my cousin who came and ironed for hours

… a friend who washed down my porch for me

… the people who stopped me in the street and said, "We are praying for your son"

… and then there was the man who worked with Barry but did not know Michael, who came to our house on a really wet Sunday and gave Michael the little homemade wooden box, (still wet with linseed oil) that held a small Good News Bible. [28]

Here are some more ideas from grieving people of how friends can make a difference. We don't need to do extraordinary things. What may seem insignificant, or what occurs spontaneously, is often what is remembered most.

Do bring casseroles – but in plastic containers for freezing. Or in an attractive dish for serving – and don't expect your friend to return it.

Make your own cuppa when visiting.

Volunteer to get clothes dry cleaned or shoes polished or pick up friends who are arriving for the funeral.

Bring practical things that are going to be needed if the house is full of visitors – toilet paper, paper plates, napkins, ice for drinks.

Wash the car, do the ironing, walk the dog, weed the garden – don't just say, "If there's anything I can do give me a call." How many people do you know who would ring up and say, "Come over and do the cleaning. I just can't face it."

The morning after our baby died we went off to arrange the funeral. When we got back home my neighbour had been and washed the load of nappies that signalled a baby used to live here. I was so glad she did that. It was the last thing I felt like doing.

Visit or phone three, six, nine and twelve months later. You can bet you'll be one of the few who still bother.

A friend collected all the spent flowers from the arrangements which were sent to our house. She then dried them and made them into potpourri which was given back to us in a jar.

Someone gave us a video with year by year segments of our get togethers and holidays in it. It was hard to look at in the beginning but now I'm really glad I've got it.

My friend organised a BBQ on the first anniversary and she brought the beetroot – because my husband never had a barbie without beetroot.

It was our daughter's birthday a few months after our baby died. I just couldn't face organising a party so a friend did it instead; the cake, the party games, and the washing up afterwards.

It helps to know your friends are there with you each day, helping to look after the rest of the family, doing the things you CANNOT and DON'T want to do anymore.

Saying to somebody "let me know if there is anything I can do" is just infuriating. If I knew how to help myself don't you think I would've done it by now!

The best support was when people just did stuff because ... like dropping around food because they had made extra. Booking tickets to movies or arranging social occasions. It was good to feel included but also free to just be if you weren't up to it on the day. Friends that acknowledged birthdays and anniversaries, even just commenting that there will be an empty seat at the Christmas table this year. People that chose not to ignore the loss and felt comfortable acknowledging the change his absence had on my life.

When I was having treatment for my breast cancer, I kept a daily journal for almost a year – it was my trusted companion – the place where I felt safe to be honest about how I was really doing.

Here is my entry on July 12, 2013:

I've just come back home from radiation, it's number 27 today. My chest looks like it's been hit by a blow torch and I have to wash my car because it's driving me nuts that it hasn't been washed in months. But everyone says, "If there's anything I can do, just give me a call." As if I'm going to ask someone to wash my car, surely they can see it needs a wash!

Rather than waiting to be asked, here is a list of some of the ways my friends found to show they cared and they wanted to help – spontaneous, generous, creative.

- *Every 3 weeks when a new round of chemo began, my school friend since we were 11 years old sent a small gift in the mail to brighten my day – pretty soap, note paper, a CD, some nice tea, hand cream.*

- *When I hardly felt like eating anything, my neighbour enquired if I'd like some chicken soup for dinner that night; it arrived all bubbly and hot, already served in a bowl, ready to eat. No cooking required.*

- *I phoned another neighbour to ask if I could have some of her aloe vera for my burnt skin. She not only brought me a piece, but planted an entire plant in my garden so that I had a ready supply.*

- *A male colleague said he would shave his head in sympathy if I lost my hair – sure enough, he kept his word and sent me a photo as proof.*

- *A friend cooked tiny meals, packaged them in plastic containers – with a motivational quote stuck to each lid just to keep my thoughts on track.*

- *Another friend wrote regular newsy letters always ending with a message saying "no need to write back, save your energy".*

- *A colleague sent intermittent SMS photos of beautiful sunrises from his waterfront home, no message attached, no words needed.*

- *I was given a mantra by a Buddhist nun for the down days: May I be well. May I be happy. May I be peaceful.*

- *A complete stranger watched me buying some hats in winter to cover my bald head. She insisted on knitting me some and as promised they arrived in the mail a few weeks later.*

- *My younger brother, the family comedian, who had a heart attack a few weeks after my cancer diagnosis, sent me a cartoon with this well-known quote; "What doesn't kill you, makes you stronger!" This became our private joke – only he could get away with saying something like that. Even if you've got cancer, you can still have a sense of humour!*

- *A friend sent me an array of natural skin care products – just reading the ingredients made me feel better – aromatic botanicals, softening jojoba, soothing aloe vera, hydrating rosehip – just what I needed to be kind to my body.*

- *My sister came to stay several times, not for conversation, but for company – she insisted I needn't sit around talking to her, she just wanted to be there to keep an eye on me. I learned just 'being' is actually 'doing' enough.*

- *A work colleague in New Zealand signed off his get well message with the words 'Kia Kaha'. I didn't know what they meant but thanks to Google I learned that these words originate from a Maori phrase meaning 'stay strong'. When the 2011 earthquake hit Christchurch, 'Kia Kaha' became an iconic message used by the Maori and pakeha (European) people alike to give solace and comfort and a sense of unity to the people of the city. These words just resonated with me. They didn't say 'be brave', or 'don't cry', they just said you have the strength inside you to get through this. I wanted to be counted amongst those people who knew how to survive adversity.*

There's something else you can do which is equally as helpful as words or deeds. It's touch. A hug can convey a message that might otherwise not sound true if you're searching for the 'right' words. A squeeze of the hand or a supportive arm around a shoulder need no extra words. Be mindful though, that some people are uncomfortable when others get too close. You will have to trust your instinct and common sense to judge what's right. Having said this, I have spoken with countless bereaved people who agree that if you don't know what to say, then a hug will convey it for you. Or simply say, "I don't know what to say to you, but I want to know what I can do to help you".

Of all the things which happened, no more caring gesture comes to mind than that of my father. At Tristan's grave side he put his hand on my shoulder. Dad is not an expressive man and his physical gestures had always been punitive in my childhood. His touch means a great deal to me to this day.

I would advise any care giver to invest in touching. If only more of the people who (so obviously) cared for me had put a hand on me or even so much as stood in my personal space or met my gaze evenly and without flinching, I would have drawn great strength. Touching is 'dangerous' for males – I must admit I would not have practised what I now preach. I do now. For men or women who are too reserved for touching, I would urge them to simply confess inadequacy and thereafter, at regular intervals, enquire about such matters as health, sleep, eating – take a direct and personal interest in the bereaved's personal life without pretending to hold any magic formula for removing the grief – it's far better than silent awkwardness or ignorance.

I remember becoming upset while telling a group of people about her death. The man next to me very quietly took my hand and squeezed it. He held the grip (or was it me?) until I stopped crying. He said nothing and yet he said everything.

Don't stand back. Admit your inability to fully understand. Hold. Listen. Touch. Even laugh when appropriate. Just be there and be yourself.

You can make your friend's grief more bearable, but not fix it, by staying in touch as the months go by, knowing that many others will be making noises about getting on with the future and not living in the past. You, on the other hand, now know that a large part of your friend's future will be concerned with how well they deal with the events of the past, not how quickly they try to forget them.

You can endorse the idea of 'continuing bonds' – letting your friend know that it's okay to keep the person 'alive' in their thoughts and at those times when they feel they want them to be acknowledged. Here are some ideas of how others have done this:

AFL footy is my passion and Glen's passion was Rugby League so I go to a game where his favourite team is playing be it here in Queensland or in NSW or sometimes I can fluke a game in Melbourne against The Storm.

Spiritually I have a chunk of Rose Quartz beside my bed and when I want to talk to Glen I just rub the stone and start talking or venting in some cases, but this helps me to feel connected still.

I have my own box of stuff (that's what people would call it if they could see it) but to me it is those memories and letters, emails and Glen things (my anger letters/notes to Glen are in there as well, the good, bad and ugly box).

On his first anniversary I had my soda water drink and bought his favourite bottle of beer and sat down on the beach and drank my water and poured out his beer into the sand.

I like to remember my brother Steve when bike riding. This is something we both enjoyed. In 2014 my then 8-year-old daughter Eliza, my dad and I did the Great Victorian Bike Ride. A huge feat for Eliza to cycle 180km in 3 days. During this time and in our training it was really nice to reflect with my dad on his experience doing other Great Victorian Bike Rides with Steve. Simple chats about what the food was like, the heat they experienced one year and torrential rain another year all bought back memories and helped me continue my bond with my brother and share my expression of that love with Eliza.

Eliza had another uncle (her dad's brother) who passed away when I was 8 months pregnant with her. Uncle Milos was blind and remarkably did the Great Victorian Bike Ride on a tandem bike. While we were riding, Eliza asked many questions about how Milos could have done what she was doing as a blind person. It put Milos in context for her as a real person she could relate to. Milos gave me a teddy bear for Eliza before he went into his final surgery that he did not recover from. This teddy bear could only have been selected by someone without sight as it's the softest bear ever and holds great sentiment to Eliza and is treated with a level of care – greater than another possession.

Eliza was born on my brother Steve's birthday. I've always made a point to make her birthday about her and not Steve but every night when I tuck her in to bed I have a song I sing to her that's an adapted Christmas carol that goes, "little baby Eliza born on Stephen's day". This ritual gives Eliza great comfort, probably because of the attention, back rub and mummy time but it also comforts me because I get to hear my brother's name and have him part of my day.

I wear my mother's wedding ring and each night before I go to sleep, I hold my hands together and enclose the ring on my finger. I send her a quiet message of love and gratitude and maybe a funny remembrance, and for that brief moment, we are together. Then I go to sleep. I am honouring her memory and continuing the bond. What a gift.

I'm often asked if it's wrong to get upset yourself when a friend is crying. I don't believe your friend expects you to be anything other than natural – so if you're sad too it's okay to show it. It's only a problem if your friend has to put their tears on hold so that they can comfort you.

I would say this also applies to people like health professionals, clergy and funeral directors. Their patients or clients do not expect any super human show of strength that prevents them from being affected by the grief of others. If you do become emotional it's important to recognise why – are you upset because of your friend or patient's sadness or has this event triggered something inside you that you've suppressed or that's happening in your own life right now? You need to work out the difference so that you can get some help for yourself if that's the case.

One of the most tender moments I have witnessed was the sight of a doctor, in a hospital ward, cradling a child in his arms who had just died. He stroked the child's hair, his face wet with tears. The child's parents whispered to me, "He loved her too".

This doctor's tears tell us something else as well – caring does not happen without some kind of toll on the carer or helper. It's hard work making yourself available to someone who needs to offload a pile of emotions. This means you will require some self-care of your own, otherwise your level of helpfulness will begin to dwindle. Practical ways to do this include designated free time for yourself, especially if you have just had a long visit or phone call with a grieving person. Fresh air, your favourite music, relaxation, a massage, some exercise or any other way you like to 'spoil yourself' can give you back the energy you need to keep your own life in order. Time for yourself is not selfish.

Sometimes, you may even have to tell your grieving friend that right now is just not a suitable time for you to talk, especially if you expect the conversation to go on for some time. Saying "no" is your right and need not offend if it is said in a way that conveys you still care. Perhaps something like this could be adapted when you need to attend to your own priorities:

I can tell that you're really lonely at the moment but I was just about to bath the kids. Could I call you back when I've got them into bed and then I can talk to you without any interruptions?

OR

It sounds like you're having one of those bad days. I wish I could talk to you about it now but I have to get this report finished by lunch time. Can I suggest we meet after work and go somewhere for a coffee and then I know I can give you all of my attention?

OR

Gee, you've caught me at a bad time. I feel awkward asking this but can we talk just for a few minutes now, and then have a real catch up tomorrow?

The important components of the above statements are that they all indicate to the bereaved that their need is being heard, even though the time is not available to attend to it adequately at the moment. Secondly, by organising another meeting time, the helper is indicating that his concern is indeed genuine. Most grieving people would be able to see that they weren't being ignored and would be open to negotiating a suitable time to get together.

CHAPTER 12

AT A GLANCE

- Helpers don't just offer help and then are never seen ... as well as being there to listen, they look for ways to lessen the burden of the household needs, they roll up their sleeves, they turn up.

- Helpers know that a touch on the arm, a hug or just being there in silence counts too.

- Helpers think up their own ideas on how to help ... they don't expect their friend to come up with ways to lighten their load.

- Keeping company with grieving people can be tiring. Listening itself is hard work. Helpers need to remember to care for themselves too, and when necessary put limits on their availability.

- Helpers are there for the long haul, and they realise that it feels good when their friend knows they can openly share their ongoing thoughts, memories and connections with them.

CHAPTER 13

OVER TO YOU – HOW WOULD YOU RESPOND WITH EMPATHY?

You will have the idea by now that talking to someone you know who is grieving is not an exercise in finding a whole lot of words designed to cheer up the person. And you will be aware of the danger of choosing the wrong words:

Remember to whom you are talking. Comments such as 'Men are bastards', although throw away lines, are very cutting to someone who is desperate to have her man back.

It's okay to say, "I can't imagine how you feel" – no, you probably can't and that's how it should be. No one should go looking for hell.

Don't say, "It would be worse to lose a child." It may be, but I don't give a shit.

I will never forget people talking all the time about trivial things like washing, cooking, other people and THEIR families, THEIR sons. That used to hurt me so much. I thought how insensitive they were.

When you don't know what to say sometimes it's best just to shut up. Words are not everything. Actions are more important. When someone dies they are gone forever. Those left behind want to remember forever. Good friends commit to that journey of being there forever.

Helping is based on communication – either through words or actions that say you recognise the loss, hear the grief and are willing to share the load. It's unrealistic to think you can do much more or that your friend expects much more from you. Arm yourself with the tools that will help you keep conversations relevant and beneficial: second-chance questions, mentioning the name of the person who died, listening more and talking less, knowing how to empathise to show you understand, communicating with eye contact or touch, conquering your own fears about talking about feelings and 'putting your foot in it', understanding why you don't have to have the answers or fancy words or clichés to brighten up the conversation, allowing your friend more than a couple of months to be 'back on track' and remembering significant days and the memory triggers that can trip them up at any time.

Now it's over to you. Here is an opportunity for you to practise your listening and empathy.

There are 10 extracts from the real words of grieving people and you are asked to give a helpful, empathetic response. I suggest you try to write more than one response, so that you demonstrate that empathetic responses are not like well-established one-line clichés. They sound like natural conversation.

They show how you have picked up on the meaning of another's story – remember, I've called that the 'essence' of what they wanted me to know and understand. Your response leaves the door open for the conversation to continue because the speaker's grief isn't stopped in its tracks by a response that is inappropriate to their story.

To guide you, here are some statements with an empathetic quality and you can see how varied each one is.

- It sounds like you're feeling really …

- I can see how much that's hurt you.

- I can understand why you're so upset. He/she meant the world to you.

- You're really lost without him/her. Life's just not the same anymore for you.

- I sense there's a great big hole in your life that nothing can fill.

- You're feeling so empty inside.

- Your life's been turned upside down.

- Your head's full of questions and nothing seems to make any sense.

- You sound like you want to turn the clock back and say ...

- It seems like you're really struggling with this ...

- It's hard to understand why the world keeps turning when your own life seems to have stopped.

Remember, your role is to:

- Listen to their inventory – listen compassionately, let them tell you whatever is on their mind.

- Hear what matters most – why are they telling me this? What is the essence of their message?

- Give them permission to have their grief – it's alright to feel the way they do.

- Stay with their feelings – don't avoid their grief or change the subject.

- Accept and understand – your response needs to show you get the picture, you're on their wavelength – you have heard how it is for them.

You can compare your answers with the suggested responses at the end of the chapter.

CHAPTER 13

AT A GLANCE

- Help can come from counsellors, God, relatives, workmates, strangers, friends and YOU. Remember, it's not who you are, but how you respond – in words and actions that will be the measure of your ability to say or do what is effective and truly supportive when someone you know is grieving.

- Helpers recognise that whilst loss is around us everywhere, each individual has their own story to tell when it happens to them.

- Helpers know that part of their role is to share the load their friend is carrying, so they must be prepared to share the pain. It's their contribution to the friendship.

- Helpers aim to see the world the way their grieving friend does.

1. Lorraine

Lorraine's 20-year-old son Michael died in 1983, two years after being diagnosed with leukaemia. Ten years after his death, she released a very honest and detailed book telling of her family's experience both during his illness and in the aftermath of his death. [29]

Lorraine says:

… we had been invited to attend one of our friend's daughter's wedding. We struggled with our emotions, as we both didn't feel too good, but felt it would look sort of rude if we did not attend. "What would our excuse be?" we asked ourselves. That our hearts were too heavy? Would anyone understand that? We wondered.

We finally accepted the wedding invitation and put ourselves through another agony. We were reminded that our darling Michael never graced the altar rails and we see girls and boys his age, and we cry inwardly. We made it to the reception, both of us appearing that all was well. As soon as the speeches were finished, music started and touched the very chords of my heart. Barry, who had not said how he felt, just touched me on the arm, and said, "Come on, let's go."

We gave our apologies to our hosts and said goodbye. They were surprised we were going home so early saying, "We thought you would have enjoyed yourself tonight!"

We did not speak on the way home, and went straight to our bedroom and sat on the end of the bed.

We both burst out crying together, and promised we would not put ourselves through that ever again.

Ask yourself: what is the essence of this story?

....

....

....

....

....

....

....

....

....

You respond with empathy saying:

....

....

....

....

....

....

....

....

....

2. David

David Bennett wrote about his experience and what he learned when he was diagnosed with colon cancer in 2003, aged 65. In his book, Cancer for Two: conquering a cancer together, *he described the medical sequence and issues of his cancer and the emotional consequences for him and his wife, Ann.*[30]

David says:

The waiting was over. On a hot Friday morning, the day before the operation, I was at Cabrini Hospital at 11.30 am for final X-rays and admission as a patient ...

That morning, I felt sorry for Ann and my family. I am sure that, in comparable situations, this would be a common reaction for the person with the primary problem. I had a strong feeling of regret about causing the strain and worry for my wife and family. I was also very mindful that, on the next day, Ann would be waking up alone in a silent house. If the operation did not go well, or if what the surgeon found about the extent of the cancer was disappointing, Ann, alone there, was in for an anxious and difficult time. I decided to send her flowers, timed to arrive on the morning of my operation. I thought that the most appropriate choice would be some Australian flowers in bright summer colours, but these were not easy to choose over the telephone.

Then, before we were due to leave for the hospital, Ann had to go out for a short time. During that time, I took the opportunity to walk to a local florist to choose the flowers. I asked the florist to deliver the flowers to Ann early on the next day, privately intending that she should receive them before the operation had ended. On the card to accompany them, it was simple to express what I wanted to say but, as I pushed the card over the counter towards the florist, I was very conscious of why this delivery was even necessary. I felt a surge of emotion tighten my throat and make it difficult to speak. I realised once again that my feelings were deeper than I could readily recognise or acknowledge to myself.

Ask yourself: what is the essence of this story?

....

....

....

....

....

....

....

....

....

....

You respond with empathy saying:

....

....

....

....

....

....

....

....

....

....

3. Valerie

Valerie Volk has published a collection of poems – a moving and personal account of her husband Noel's impending death and her grief both before and after. Writing poetry became a means of self expression and survival for her. This poem is titled Driving Away. [31]

Valerie says:

I said goodbye to friends, walked to the car,
felt suddenly alone, bereft.

If we had been together, I'd be standing
irked, because you never would get out the keys,
release the central locking, until we were right there
and waiting.
I'd get annoyed, bite back words of irritation
Because I knew there must be many little things
I did that irked you like that too.
There always will be tiny rifts, annoyances,
the molehills that, unchecked, will soon make mountains,
unless there is an overarching tenderness
that sweeps the trivia to one side,
and recognises pebbles in the path
have power to make the trek precarious.

If we had been together, now we'd glance,
well-practised in accord, in understanding of each other.
"Coffee?" one of us would say. The other nod,
and soon we'd be enclosed within our private world
at some small coffee bar, content to be alone,
just with each other.

If we had been together, I'd not be standing here
beside the open car, with sharp tears welling,
wishing only to be irritated by you slowly, slowly,
hunting for the keys …

Ask yourself: what is the essence of this story?

....

....

....

....

....

....

....

....

....

....

You respond with empathy saying:

....

....

....

....

....

....

....

....

....

....

....

....

4. Michael

In 2015, Michael Tippet won the Hunter Writers Centre Members' Prize for his reflection on the death of his 3-year-old daughter. The following is an extract from his story, titled Cherub. [32]

Michael says:

Watching you grow was a delight. Each day delivered a magic show and I was enthralled by even your simplest trick ... barely three years old and already glimpses of the remarkable woman you would become ...

If not for the horror of that day.

Your heart, your precious heart, too great and insuppressible to be contained in a body so delicate. My memory of the events that followed is patchy at best. But I do remember the calls. The animal sounds that roared and howled in my ear as I phoned everyone that ever loved you and broke them.

Now I am Death, the destroyer of worlds.

Your mother and I left the hospital sometime later, returning to a home haunted by a pervasive absence. The new quiet was deafening.

Your bedroom was now a museum, full of exhibits left to gather dust amongst the fossilised remains of bedtime stories, good night kisses and dreams that would never be realised. Outside, our backyard had become a graveyard. Orphaned toys stuck out of the grass like cheap plastic tombstones. In a corner, the sun-faded crypt of a cubby house had been hastily abandoned.

Thirteen months have passed and I still wait for you to twirl out of your room, weaving worlds in your head and inviting me to be part of them.

There are times when I worry the hurt will never leave. The only thing that scares me more is perhaps one day it will. That somehow the easing of your loss will signify the fading of your memory, and I'll soon forget the details of your perfect cherub face.

Ask yourself: what is the essence of this story?

....

....

....

....

....

....

....

....

....

....

You respond with empathy saying:

....

....

....

....

....

....

....

....

....

....

5. Jenny

Jennifer Anne Ryan, aged 15, wrote this poem about her father's death when she was just five years old. It was found amongst her personal treasures by her mother, after Jenny sadly died in an accident as she was riding her bicycle home from school. [33]

Jenny says:

It was the year 1977, the first day of September,
For this is the day I'll always remember,
The year the day I will never forget,
And look upon it with sad regret,
For this is the day my father died,
It wasn't until years later that I cried,
And when he died I was only five,
I didn't understand the word survive,
Survive he didn't … die he did,
And when he died I was only a kid,
Dead at thirty-eight years of age,
My heart broke with anger and rage,
Why did he die, why was it so?
No one could tell me, they didn't know,
They said: 'The good die young. The bad live on.'
If he was bad he wouldn't have gone,
Ten years later and yet still I cry,
I didn't get a chance to say good-bye,
But in my mind you live on,
My love for you is an everlasting bond,
Although you were sick for many a year,
Not once did you show me your dying fear,
Even though you're gone to a different place,
Never in my life shall I forget your face.

Ask yourself: what is the essence of this story?

....
....
....
....
....
....
....
....
....
....

You respond with empathy saying:

....
....
....
....
....
....
....
....
....
....
....

6. Paulette

Paulette Keen wrote a personal account of her experience of caring for her much loved mother Beryl who had dementia. Her story was written as much as a tribute to her mother, as it was an account of how dementia affects the whole family on a day by day basis. [34]

Paulette says:

We knew that she would never be able to live independently again, and because mum could not understand what was happening, we had to go through the whole process of selling her apartment, and not being able to tell her as she could not understand or comprehend what was happening.

It was a terrible time of sadness and loss, things would never be the same again for mum, or us. Because we had never done this before, we had no idea what was involved in finding a suitable nursing home.

I turned down quite a few that were offered to us and was ostracised for my efforts ... could they not understand this was a 'real' person and not just a number? How could I send her just anywhere? I was left to defend why I loved my mother so much and how dare I refuse the offer of a nursing home that I deemed not suitable for her. It was simple, there was a benchmark/standard that I expected my mother to have and deserved and I was not willing to go below that. I visited Mum twice a day, every day, and virtually looked after her, plus helping other ladies in a similar position ...

I felt so nervous the day we moved her from hospital to nursing home, she had been wearing nighties for six months, so I packed all her dresses, dressing her in a favourite, wondering if she would remember it ... I think (hope) so. I followed in the car while she was transported by ambulance, I felt like I was taking my little child to their first day at school, knowing I would have to leave her there to fend for herself.

Ask yourself: what is the essence of this story?

....

....

....

....

....

....

....

....

....

....

You respond with empathy saying:

....

....

....

....

....

....

....

....

....

....

7. Deb

Deb Rae and her husband Stu were enjoying their lives as English teachers in Poland when an accident took Stu's life. At the age of 36 she was widowed. She has written about this life changing experience in a comprehensive 'how to survive' book directed at young widows. [35]

Deb says:

My husband was a great cook and I took full advantage of his passion and skills. My culinary knowledge dwindled significantly during our marriage and we were both just fine with that. After he died though, I was reduced to eating baked beans and chocolate bars for a while. As the cook, Stu did most of the grocery shopping. When I attempted it by myself, I couldn't remember what brand of soy sauce we used to buy, which ham was our favourite or what cheese he used to put in the lasagne. I wandered around like a lost child for a while, then went back to the chocolate aisle.

Getting the right brand of soy sauce isn't such a big deal. But it's yet another uncertainty, another thing you have to work out, another decision you have to guess at. It gets added to the steadily growing pile of stuff you have to deal with. It's like the ironing pile – a living breathing organism that could swallow an unwary adult whole. You look at it, sigh and close the laundry door, deciding to work it out later.

For some widows, the pile of stuff they need to work out gets dangerously close to exploding. There's just no space to squeeze one more little thing on top of the pile and quickly shut the door again. The widow's overloaded brain is at bursting point, and it could be the soy sauce that pushes her over the edge, right there in Aisle Six.

Feeling constantly pushed to deal with just one more new thing can be debilitating, and exhausted young widows may get very strong urges to simply give up. Let the kitchen flood, who cares about the knocking noise in the car and to hell with the soy sauce. The overwhelm gets expressed in lots of different ways – some young widows get very angry (I was very keen to knock every bottle of soy sauce off the shelves), some collapse on the kitchen floor (or cry in the shower) and others just go to bed for a long time.

Ask yourself: what is the essence of this story?

....

....

....

....

....

....

....

....

....

....

You respond with empathy saying:

....

....

....

....

....

....

....

....

....

....

8. Mary

Mary Bingham has lost her daughter to drugs. But she is still alive. Mary writes about the heartache of being powerless as a mother to impact her daughter's choices and lifestyle. [36]

Mary says:

Today I had a call from the young woman who used to be my kind and loving daughter …

"Hi Mum!"

"Hello darling, how are you today?"

"Fine. Can I borrow your car? I need to pick up my stuff from a friend's place."

I take a deep breath before I can even bear to answer. "How about I drive you there, and I can help you pick it up?"

She hangs up.

My car, covered in the scars inflicted the many times I gave in to her tearful or enraged demands, spends another day carrying groceries, not drugs, nor the dealers of these terrible substances that took my Lizzie away and replaced her with this paranoid, angry and permanently damaged young girl.

I gently put down the phone, go upstairs to my bedroom and scream into my pillow …

Every single day, this strange and scary young woman reminds me that I lost my darling daughter over ten years ago to a terrible addiction. She looks almost the same (apart from the dreadful scars that cover her face from years of ice abuse), but every time I see her there is less and less of the bright, happy girl with a heart a mile wide that was the child Elizabeth.

Ask yourself: what is the essence of this story?

....

....

....

....

....

....

....

....

....

....

You respond with empathy saying:

....

....

....

....

....

....

....

....

....

....

9. Michelle

Michelle is the loving owner of Shoki, her cat for 18 years. Through these words, she describes her last day with Shoki before taking her back to the vet to be euthanased. [37]

Michelle says:

"I didn't leave her side for 24 hours. I fed her water with a syringe. I gave her everything she wanted. Smoked salmon, ice cream, kangaroo meat. I helped her to her sand box. I put her on our bed, we talked and she purred.

I couldn't let her go. We kept her as long as we could before we took her back to the vet …

There are still days I ache for her company. She was this space in my life, this place I could go to, she was a joy to be with and I've lost that. She knew when I was down. She'd sit with me for hours. She was my confidant …

About four or five months later we decided to get another cat. I think it was more my husband's decision, I was always so down …"

Ask yourself: what is the essence of this story?

....

....

....

....

....

....

....

....

....

....

You respond with empathy saying:

....

....

....

....

....

....

....

....

....

....

10. Doris

The following extracts come from my journals which I kept during my breast cancer treatment, 2012-2013. Journalling was a great source of therapy, and allowed me to say what I often could not share with my family and friends.

Doris says:

22/11/12

Well yesterday I found out I have breast cancer. I can't believe it, it feels like an academic word. Something you get, something I read about in the newspapers. I know I'm in shock. I've tried to tell people today ... tomorrow I'll start with the work folk. I can't write anymore. It's too hard. Too big. Too crazy. Too unbelievable.

18/12/12

Today I met with the oncologist – chemo starts 8th of January. It's so real. I have cancer. I don't want it. I don't want to be sick, tired, vomit, lose my hair.

12/7/13

Had coffee today with a colleague who said I looked better than I did when she last saw me. I've had that same comment over and over in the past couple of weeks. I summise that I must have looked pretty awful but no-one would tell me. I know in my heart that I looked sick, full of chemo, grey-faced, tired, swollen- eyed, bald, tired, tired, tired, but even I thought I didn't look too bad.

18/7/13

Today is the last day of radiation. A day to celebrate. Not a soul in my life knows how important this day is. No-one has called and said "Congrats, you made it!" It tells me breast cancer is a really lonely journey in many ways, no-one really gets it.

I bought myself a new pair of shoes on the way home from radiation, for my sore feet. My shoes happen to be red – to match my right breast which is burnt to a crisp. How else do you celebrate such a milestone?

Ask yourself: what is the essence of this story?

....

....

....

....

....

....

....

....

....

....

You respond with empathy saying:

....

....

....

....

....

....

....

....

....

....

SUGGESTED EMPATHETIC RESPONSES

1. LORRAINE

It must have been such an effort to sit through that wedding and put on a happy face just to make others feel good.

I sense you were really hurt and disappointed by your friends who had no idea why it was so hard for you to be at their daughter's wedding. It's like they had no clue what you'd been through.

Weddings and other family get-togethers are going to be tough for a long time. It's not just that Mick is missing, it's knowing that he won't reach those same milestones himself.

2. DAVID

It sounds like you had so much going on that day – worrying about Anne, the operation itself and the unknown outcome … it must have been a scary time for you.

It seems like you were concerned for everyone else in the family except yourself.

Buying those flowers meant so much to you – they weren't just another bunch of flowers, no wonder you found it hard going emotionally.

3. VALERIE

It seems like you're constantly finding yourself tripped up by one of these reminders, probably when you least expect it. You must miss him every day.

The two of you had your own way of doing coffee – I bet something as simple as going out for a coffee these days isn't the same anymore.

I sense it's not just the obvious things you miss but it's Noel's quirky habits that you miss too – it sounds like you just want him back, warts and all.

4. MICHAEL

How empty your world must be without her. So full of life one minute and then nothing … I sense all the life was sucked out of your home the day she died.

I can understand what you mean about fearing you'll forget her face – you must want to hang on to every tiny image to keep her close.

Even though thirteen months have gone by it seems like it's still hard to believe this really happened.

5. JENNY

Even though ten years have gone by you still love your Dad, and you've been thinking about him all that time ... I sense you miss him even more now than you did when you were little.

It's been hard for you growing up without a Dad – I guess the older you've become the more there is to miss about him – it hurts not to have your Dad when you need him.

It seems like you wish you could have said a proper goodbye when you were little. It must have been confusing for you trying to work out what was happening.

6. PAULETTE

You must have loved your Mum so much. There was such a close bond between the two of you.

It sounds like finding a suitable nursing home was a real nightmare and made worse when people didn't understand what you were looking for. Second best just wasn't an option for your Mum.

It must have been a hard time for you realising that you're losing your Mum right before your own eyes, bit by bit, and you can't do a thing to fix it – no matter how much you loved her.

7. DEB

Gosh, some days the frustrations must have piled up until you thought you were at breaking point.

It sounds like the things we take for granted like shopping and cooking end up being another obstacle to deal with when you're widowed. It's those little things that turn into big things!

Having to do everything on your own and having no one to lean on or just ask to do their share – must be so hard to get used to. Like there's a gaping hole where Stu used to be and no way to fill it in.

8. MARY

You've not just lost Elizabeth, you've lost all the dreams you had for your little girl and your life with her.

It's so hard for you – as a Mum you just want to be able to 'kiss it better' and make all her troubles go away. But you've found out you can't, no matter how much you love her.

The years seem to have taken their toll on you too, not just Elizabeth. Ten years is a long time to sit in the midst of all this and just watch her go down hill.

9. MICHELLE

Shoki was like a best girlfriend, always there for you. No wonder you couldn't let her go, she was one of the family.

It must have broken your heart to say goodbye. She meant the world to you.

Those last few hours were so precious. Of course you couldn't leave her side. I can see how much you loved her right to the end.

10. DORIS

Gee, that must have been a challenging time for you. It looks like your world got turned upside down and by the sound of it some days were pretty awful.

Losing your hair – what a nightmare! What about those new red shoes – looks like you didn't lose your sense of humour!

You're saying that you just didn't lose your hair. So much was going on in your whole body. I bet it was even hard to look in the mirror and see what was going on.

BIBLIOGRAPHY

1. Auon et al *Who Needs Bereavement Support? A Population Based Study of Bereavement Risk and Support Need*, PLOS ONE | DOI:10.1371/journal.pone.0121101 March 26, 2015 p.2

2. Auon et al ibid. p.4

3. Auon et al ibid. p.6

4. Thich Nhat Hanh *True Love: A Practice for Awakening the Heart*, Shambhala Boston & London, 2011 p.3

5. Griffin, Graeme *Talking About Death*, Joint Board of Christian Education of Australia and New Zealand, Melbourne 1976 pp.14-15

6. Egan, Gerard *The Skilled Helper: A Systematic Approach to Effective Helping*, Brooks/Cole Publishing Company California 1986 p.67

7. Based on a concept from Williams, Litsa *64 Myths About Grief That Just Have To STOP*, www.whatsyourgrief.com posted on August 4, 2015

8. Freud, E. L. (Ed) *Letters of Sigmund Freud*, Basic Books, New York 1961 *in* Worden, J.W. *Grief Counselling & Grief Therapy*, Springer Publishing Company Inc New York 1982 p.17

9. Williams, Litsa *Continuing Bonds: Shifting the Grief Paradigm*, www.whatsyourgrief.com posted on February 17, 2014

10. Haley, Eleanor *Grieving Styles: Intuitive and Instrumental Grief*, www.whatsyourgrief.com posted on April 28, 2015

11. Doka Ph D, Kenneth J *Disenfranchised Grief: Recognising Hidden Sorrow*, www.cruse.org.uk/.../pdf/Events/KDDisenfranchisedgrief.pdf

12. Smith, Claire Bidwell *The Rules of Inheritance*, The Text Publishing Company Australia 2012 p.234

13. Barwon Region Child Health Centre (Barwon Paediatric Unit, Geelong) *Has a Child You Loved Died? – A report of Phone-in Survey April 1986*

14. Zagdanski, Doris *When Pets Die – It's Alright to Grieve*, Michelle Anderson Publishing Pty Ltd Australia 2005 pp.66-68

15. Griffin, Graeme op. cit. p.23

16. Grennan, Lorraine *Mick…Send me a butterfly*, Lorraine Grennan 2012 p.236

17. Grennan, Lorraine ibid. pp.271-272

18. Stanfield, Elaine *Silent Grief – Certain Hope: Words of Encouragement and Comfort*, Out of Our Minds Publishing Australia 2014 p.18

19. Khoshaba Psy.D., Deborah *About Complicated Bereavement Disorder*, https://www.psychologytoday.com/blog/get-hardy/201309

20. Grennan, Lorraine op. cit. pp.288-289

21. Commonwealth of Australia *LIFE Living is for everyone: Factsheet 23 I know someone who is suicidal*, www.livingisforeveryone.com.au 2007

22. Commonwealth of Australia *LIFE Living is for everyone: Factsheet 21 Suicide warning signs and tipping points*, www.livingisforeveryone.com.au 2007

23. Grennan, Lorraine op. cit. p.238

24. Grennan, Lorraine op. cit. p.243

25. Lord, Janet Deveson *When A Baby Suddenly Dies*, Hill Of Content Publishing Company Melbourne 1987 pp.194-197

26. Zagdanski, Doris *Teenagers and Grief,* Michelle Anderson Publishing Pty Ltd Australia 2012 Edition pp.20-27

27. Irizarry Ph. D., Carol *Children and Death*, John Allison/Monkhouse Support Services Melbourne

28. Grennan, Lorraine Op Cit p.262

29. Grennan, Lorraine Op Cit p.252-253

30. Bennett, David *Cancer For Two: conquering a cancer together,* Michelle Anderson Publishing Pty Ltd Australia 2006 pp.54-56

31. Volk, Valerie *In Due Season: Poems of love and loss,* Pantaenus Press 2009 p.62

32. Tippett, Michael *Cherub* in *Grieve: Stories and Poems for Grief Awareness Month 2015,* Hunter Writers Centre 2015 pp.15-16

33. Zagdanski, Doris *Teenagers and Grief,* Michelle Anderson Publishing Pty Ltd Australia 2012 Edition p.105

34. Keen, Paulette *Precious Beryl ... a Legacy: Understanding Dementia ...one life, one view*

35. Rae, Deb *Getting there – grief to peace for young widows,* Deb Rae 2015 p.159

36. Bingham, Mary *Losing Elizabeth* in *Grieve: Stories and Poems for Grief Awareness Month 2015,* Hunter Writers Centre 2015 p.7

37. Zagdanski, Doris *When Pets Die – It's Alright to Grieve,* Michelle Anderson Publishing Pty Ltd Australia 2005 pp.64-65

ACKNOWLEDGEMENTS

First and foremost, I am indebted to all the grieving people, young and old, male and female, who shared their stories, spoke their truth and have generously allowed me to colour the text with tangible, living examples of the impact of loss and grief in their lives.

The following publishers, authors and organisations have kindly granted permission to quote from their works:

Barwon Region Child Health Centre (Barwon Paediatric Unit, Geelong) *Has a Child You Loved Died? – A report of Phone-in Survey April 1986*

David Bennett *Cancer For Two: conquering a cancer together*

Deb Rae *Getting there – grief to peace for young widows*

Dr Carol Irizarry & John Allison/Monkhouse Support Services *Children and Death*

Elaine Stanfield *Silent Grief – Certain Hope: Words of Encouragement and Comfort*

Joint Board of Christian Education of Australia and New Zealand – *Talking About Death* by Graeme Griffin

Lorraine Grennan *Mick … Send me a butterfly*

Maureen McCormack – poems: *Letter To A Lost One* and *You're Not There*

Hill of Content Publishing *When A Baby Suddenly Dies* by Janet Deveson Lord

Hunter Writers Centre, NSW *Grieve: Stories and Poems for Grief Awareness Month 2015*

Mary Bingham *Losing Elizabeth*

Michael Tippet *Cherub*

Paulette Keen *Precious Beryl … A Legacy: Understanding Dementia … one life, one view*

The Text Publishing Company Australia *The Rules of Inheritance* by Claire Bidwell Smith

Valerie Volk *In Due Season: Poems of love and loss*

Finally, over many years, amongst my family, friends and colleagues, I have been blessed with a circle of 'compassionate listeners', whose empathy has made all the difference.

NOW THAT THE FUNERAL IS OVER

"Do not walk around the edge of your grief", says Doris Zagdanski, in this common sense guide for grieving people.

Grief is often described as the 'normal and natural' response to loss. Yet, when it happens to us, we often feel like we're going crazy and there's nothing normal about our world right now. And so begins a time of change, re-organisation and adaptation.

In this book, Doris describes the ups and downs of grief. There are no stages or phases to follow, just your 'grief work' to do. And as you turn each page, there is an inspirational thought to guide you along.

And if you know someone who's grieving, learn why you don't have to fix it or try to take their pain away. Find out the right response to anger, guilt or "why me?"

A small book that is big on wisdom, strategies and helpful ideas.

www.wilkinsonpublishing.com